Shire County

GW00362830

SUSSEX

David J. Allen

Shire Publications Ltd

2

Published in 1995 by Shire Publications Ltd, Cromwell House, Church Street, Princes Risborough, Buckinghamshire HP27 9AA, UK.
Copyright © 1984 and 1995 by David J. Allen. First published 1984. Second edition 1987. Third edition 1995. Shire County Guide 4. ISBN 0 7478 0272 6.

Printed in Great Britain by CIT Printing Services, Press Buildings, Merlins Bridge, Haverford-west, Dyfed SA61 1XF.

British Library Cataloguing in Publication Data
Allen, David J.
Sussex. – 3 Rev. ed. – (Shire County Guides; No. 4)
I. Title II. Series
914.22504859
ISBN 0-7478-0272-6

Acknowledgements

All the photographs are by the author. The county maps and town plans are by Robert Dizon.

Ordnance Survey grid references

Although information on how to reach most of the places described in this book by car is given in the text, National Grid References are also included in many instances, particularly for the harder-to-find places in chapters 3 and 4, for the benefit of those readers who have the Ordnance Survey 1:50,000 Landranger maps of the area. The references are stated as a Landranger sheet number followed by the 100 km National Grid square and the six-figure reference.

To locate a site by means of the grid references, proceed as in the following example: Woods Mill (OS 198: TQ 218138). Take the OS Landranger map sheet 198 ('Brighton and the Downs'). The grid numbers are printed in blue around the edges of the map. In more recently produced maps these numbers are repeated at 10 km intervals throughout the map, so that it is not necessary to open it out completely. Read off these numbers from the left along the top edge of the map until you come to 21, denoting a vertical grid line, then estimate eight-tenths of the distance to vertical line 22 and envisage an imaginary vertical grid line 21.8 at this point. Next look at the grid numbers at one side of the map (either side will do) and read *upwards* until you find the horizontal grid line 13. Estimate eight-tenths of the distance to the next horizontal line above (i.e. 14), and so envisage an imaginary horizontal line across the map at 13.8. Follow this imaginary line across the map until it crosses the imaginary vertical line 21.8. At the intersection of these two lines you will find Woods Mill.

The Ordnance Survey Landranger maps which cover Sussex are sheets 186, 187, 188, 189, 197, 198 and 199.

Cover: *The chalk cliffs and lighthouse at Beachy Head.*

Contents

4

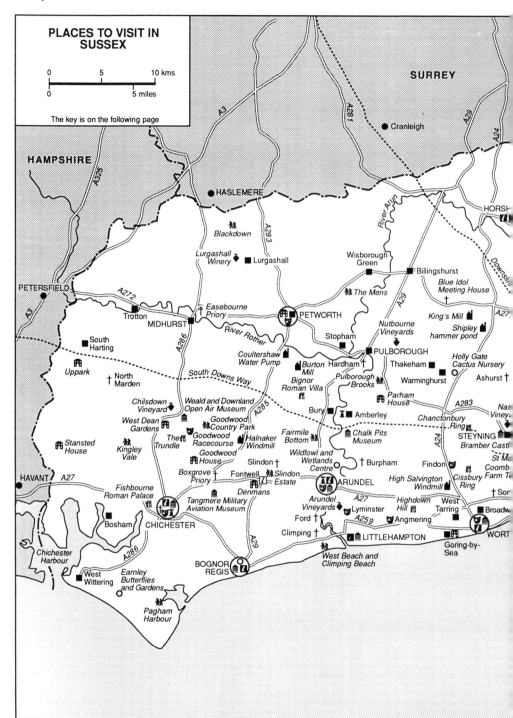

PLACES TO VISIT IN SUSSEX

0   5   10 kms

0   5 miles

The key is on the following page

SURREY

HAMPSHIRE

Cranleigh

HASLEMERE

Blackdown

Lurgashall Winery

Lurgashall

Wisborough Green

Billingshurst

Blue Idol Meeting House

The Mens

PETERSFIELD

Easebourne Priory

Trotton

MIDHURST

River Rother

PETWORTH

King's Mill

Nutbourne Vineyards

Stopham

Shipley hammer pond

South Harting

Uppark

North Marden

South Downs Way

Coultershaw Water Pump

Burton Mill

Hardham

PULBOROUGH

Thakeham

Holly Gate Cactus Nursery

Bignor Roman Villa

Pulborough Brooks

Warminghurst

Ashurst

Chilsdown Vineyard

Weald and Downland Open Air Museum

Bury

Parham House

A283

West Dean Gardens

Goodwood Country Park

Amberley

Chanctonbury Ring

Nas Viney

Stansted House

Kingley Vale

The Trundle

Goodwood Racecourse

Halnaker Windmill

Fairmile Bottom

Chalk Pits Museum

STEYNING

Bramber Castl

St Ma

Goodwood House

Slindon

Wildfowl and Wetlands Centre

Burpham

Findon

Coomb Farm Te

Cissbury Ring

HAVANT

A27

Fishbourne Roman Palace

Boxgrove Priory

Fontwell

Slindon Estate

Denmans

ARUNDEL

High Salvington Windmill

West Tarring

Sor

Bosham

CHICHESTER

Tangmere Military Aviation Museum

Arundel Vineyards

Lyminster

Highdown Hill

Broadw

WORT

Ford

Angmering

Chichester Harbour

West Wittering

Earnley Butterflies and Gardens

Clipping

LITTLEHAMPTON

Goring-by-Sea

BOGNOR REGIS

West Beach and Climping Beach

Pagham Harbour

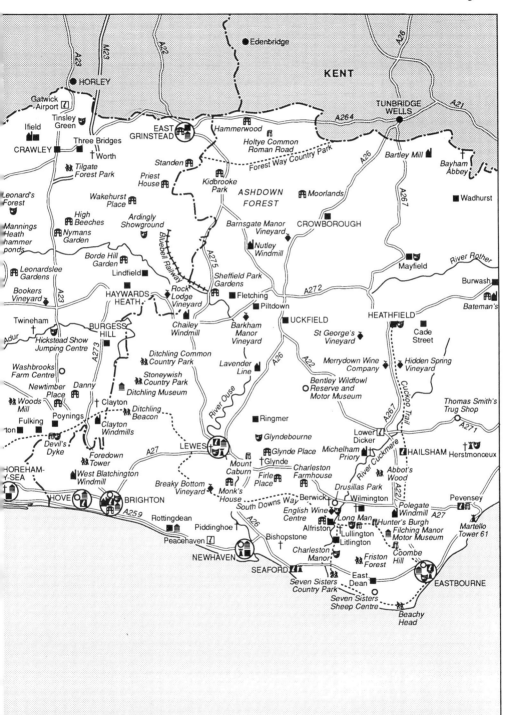

6

KENT

ASHFORD

Bayham Abbey

Cranbrook

TENTERDEN

Wadhurst
Bewl Water
Flimwell Bird Park
Ticehurst
Hawkhurst

Pashley Manor Gardens

River Rother

Haremere Hall
Bodiam Castle
Bodiam
Farm World
NEW ROMNEY

Burwash
Etchingham
Salehurst
Great Dixter
Northiam

Bateman's
Robertsbridge
Robertsbridge Abbey
Quarry Farm

A268

Brightling
Footland Wood
Sedlescombe Vineyard
RYE
Martello Tower 28

Leeford Vineyards
Brede
Camber Castle
Rye Harbour Nature Reserve

Ashburnham iron furnace
Penhurst
BATTLE
Carr Taylor Vineyards
Winchelsea
A259

Ashburnham
Fore Wood
A2100
Fairlight Country Park

Thomas Smith's Trug Shop
A271
Ninfield
A269
HASTINGS

Herstmonceux
St Leonards
A259
BEXHILL

Pevensey

Martello Tower 61

PLACES TO VISIT IN SUSSEX

- ■ Town or village (chapter 2)
- Town or village with information centre (chapters 2 and 14)
- 魏 Coast and countryside (chapter 3)
- •••• Long-distance path (chapter 3)
- Place of archaeological interest (chapter 4)
- ▲ Castle or fortification (chapter 5)
- † Ecclesiastical building (chapter 6)
- Historic house or garden (chapter 7)
- 🏛 Museum or gallery (chapter 8)
- ▲ Industrial heritage (chapter 9)
- O Other place to visit (chapter 10)
- ♦ Vineyard or wine centre (chapter 10)
- 🐛 Folklore, custom or event (chapter 11)
- Tourist information centre (chapter 14)
- ══ Principal road
- ∼ River
- ⊥⊥ Canal

0   5   10 kms

0   5 miles

Preface

Welcome to the Shire County Guide to Sussex, one of over thirty such books, written and designed to enable you to organise your time in the county well.

The Shire County Guides fill the need for a compact, accurate and thorough guide to each county so that visitors can plan a half-day excursion or a whole week's stay to best advantage. Residents, too, will find the guides a handy and reliable reference to the places of interest in their area.

Travelling British roads can be time consuming, and the County Guides will ensure that you need not inadvertently miss any interesting feature in a locality, that you do not accidentally bypass a new museum or an outstanding church, that you can find an attractive place to picnic, and that you will appreciate the history and the buildings of the towns or villages in which you stop.

This book has been arranged in special interest chapters, such as the coast and countryside, historic houses and gardens or industrial heritage, and all these places of interest are located on the map on pages 4-6. Use the map either for an overview to decide which area has most to interest you, or to help you enjoy your immediate neighbourhood. Then refer to the nearest town or village in chapter 2 to see, at a glance, what special features or attractions each community contains or is near. The subsequent chapters enable readers with a particular interest to find immediately those places of importance to them, while the cross-referencing under 'Towns and villages' assists readers with wider tastes to select how best to spend their time.

Converted oasthouses at Ewhurst Green.

1
Sussex landscapes and history

Sussex is one of the southern maritime counties of Britain and is bounded by Kent, Surrey, Hampshire and the English Channel. In 1888 the county was divided into two for administrative purposes: East Sussex, with its county town at Lewes, and West Sussex, centred on the cathedral city of Chichester.

It is not a large county, being less than 80 miles (130 km) from east to west and 30 miles (50 km) from north to south, but within this area it encompasses a wide variety of landscapes. The climate is equable and there are rarely any extremes of temperature.

Although thought of primarily for its seaside resorts, Sussex is full of surprises. It is one of the most visited counties in England, and entirely within commuting distance of London, yet many villages remain remote and relatively unknown. When the beaches and main roads are packed, almost any country lane will lead to a quiet little village.

The landscape is easy to understand since the geological formations were deposited in layers directly on top of one another, culminating in a layer of chalk several hundred feet thick. During the last cataclysmic earth movements, when the Alps were formed, these layers were forced up into a dome-shaped mass, several thousand feet high and covering much of southern England. This mass was eroded by weather and the action of rivers, and the North and South Downs are left as the outer edges of the dome. Between these chalk hills lies the Weald, an area of softer sandstones and clay, and differential erosion of these materials has resulted in deep valleys, flat clay vales and high sandstone hills which almost equal the heights of the Downs.

The county can be divided into three distinct regions: the Coastal Plain, the South Downs and the Weald.

The Coastal Plain

A roughly triangular area lying along the south coast in the western half of the county, the Coastal Plain is about 10 miles (16 km) wide at the Hampshire border and narrows to an apex at Shoreham-by-Sea 30 miles (50 km) away. To the north, the Downs form a backdrop. The flat fertile plain is an important horticultural area both for outdoor crops and for those under glass, such as tomatoes, lettuces and cut flowers. Thatched roofs are common in this area and the villages are often scattered and straggling and achieve a degree of seclusion which is surprising considering the flatness of the area.

The climate is very favourable, with high sunshine figures, and the protection of the Downs keeps temperatures higher than in many parts of Britain. The good climate and excellent beaches have resulted in the almost continuous development of the coast from Pagham Harbour eastward to Shoreham. The resorts of Bognor Regis, Littlehampton and numerous smaller ones run into one another. All have good beaches and the usual amenities but each has its own individual style.

The cathedral city of Chichester stands at the north-east corner of Chichester Harbour, 6 or 7 miles (10-12 km) from the sea in the extreme west of the county. On the eastern side of the harbour lies the Selsey peninsula, where the Romans and Saxons landed, as did St Wilfrid, who brought Christianity to Sussex. This whole coast is under constant attack from the sea and St Wilfrid's original cathedral lies under the sea. On the eastern edge of the peninsula lies Pagham Harbour, similar to Chichester Harbour, but much smaller in area.

The South Downs

The South Downs are easily the most arrest-

The South Downs near Goodwood Racecourse.

ing feature of the Sussex landscape, yet they occupy a relatively small area of the county. From the Hampshire border the Downs run south-eastward for about 55 miles (90 km), coming to an abrupt end at Beachy Head. The Downs are unlike other areas of the county; they look different, the soil has a chalk foundation found nowhere else in Sussex, and they support a variety of plant species, many of which occur only on chalk soils.

In West Sussex the chalk soil is overlaid with deposits of clay and flint; these areas are often heavily wooded, and oak trees, which rarely grow on chalk, are often present in small clumps or 'caps' which stand out clearly in open scenery. These have usually been planted, as at Chanctonbury Ring. In East Sussex the Downs are characterised by gently sloping hills covered by springy turf, grazed by sheep and interspersed with patches of scrub woodland and farmland.

Since the Second World War large areas of the Downs have been intensively farmed on an arable pattern, mainly corn, a reversal of the pre-war pattern of farming, which was almost entirely devoted to sheep. The provision of water was a problem on the top of the Downs because it drains easily through the chalk to emerge at the foot of the hills as gushing springs; to overcome this, dew ponds were created on the hills by lining shallow depressions with clay.

On the southern slopes of the Downs at Findon an annual sheep fair has been held for over two centuries. In the past many of the sheep were of the South Downs breed, which was especially bred and adapted to the downland conditions by John Ellerman of Glynde in the eighteenth century, but nowadays they are usually crossbreeds.

A distinctive feature of the Downs is the numerous dry valleys which occur; these were created by the action of water in the last ice age, when the subsoil was frozen, preventing water seeping through the chalk. A spectacular series of these valleys makes up the range of cliffs known as the Seven Sisters. Here the erosion of the chalk by the sea has presented a cross-section of this valley system that can be seen particularly well from Seaford Head across the Cuckmere valley. On the north face these dry valleys have created prominent headlands thrusting out into the Weald. Early man occupied many of these sites and the area is rich in prehistoric remains. It is still possible to see in many places the outlines of early field systems.

From the Weald, Kipling's 'blunt, bow-headed, whale-backed Downs' present the prospect of a continuous unbroken line against the sky, but the Downs are cut into five blocks by the rivers Cuckmere, Ouse, Adur and Arun. The only towns in this region are Lewes and Arundel, but there are many attractive villages, most quite small and relatively unspoilt and all in the valleys, not on the water-less high ground.

Perhaps the best way to see the Downs is from the South Downs Way, which follows the line of an ancient ridgeway track. From the path there are spectacular views to the north over the Weald and southwards to the sea.

In the short length of coast where the Downs meet the sea several towns have developed. Between Brighton and Eastbourne lie the port of Newhaven and the former port of Seaford. East of Seaford the Cuckmere river meanders through a wide valley and the mouth is flanked by the white cliffs of the Downs: Seaford Head and the Seven Sisters. Much of this area is now protected by the National Trust and East Sussex County Council.

The Weald

Lying between the North and South Downs, partly in Kent and Surrey but largely in Sussex, the Weald covers an area up to 20 miles (30 km) broad and about 70 miles (110 km) long. The Romans knew the Weald as *Silva Anderida*. They built three main roads through it from London, one to Chichester (which the Saxons later named Stane Street) and two directly south, one ending north of the Brighton area and the other ending at Lewes (see Holtye Common, page 66). They did some ironworking but built no main centre there. The Saxons began the main settlement of the great wood of Andreds Weald and started the clearance. Only a fragment of the

great forest remains but, despite the loss of thousands of trees in the hurricane-force winds of the Great Storm of October 1987, Sussex remains one of the most heavily wooded counties in Britain. The characteristic tree is the oak, which the eighteenth-century traveller Arthur Young referred to as the 'weed of the Weald'. The major roads in the region run north to south from London to the coast, whilst east-west travel is still by comparatively minor roads from which innumerable narrow lanes lead off. The Weald can be divided into four regions: the north-west, the Forest Ridge, the Southern Forest Ridges and the Low Weald.

The North-west Weald

Sussex reaches its highest point, 919 feet (280 metres), here on Blackdown, part of a sandstone massif which stretches into Surrey and Hampshire. Small-scale farming was once prevalent in this area of sandy heathland, pine wood and oaks, but where this has died out there has been an upsurge of bracken and scrub. This is a quiet country with sweeping views and a handful of unspoilt villages dotted about. Alfred, Lord Tennyson, lived on Blackdown, the view from which he described as 'Green Sussex fading into blue; with one grey glimpse of sea'. William Cobbett reacted differently: 'I have never seen the earth flung about in such a wild way', he wrote in *Rural Rides*.

Southwards from Blackdown the heaths and woodlands stretch to Midhurst, the 'capital' of the region, whilst eastward the Weald widens as the Downs fall away to the south-east. Petworth, 5 miles (8 km) to the east of Midhurst, occupies a high point where the region starts to fall away to the Coastal Plain.

The Forest Ridge

The Forest Ridge, an area of high sandstone hills, stretches eastward from Horsham for some 20 miles (30 km). Extensive forests – St Leonard's, Tilgate, Worth and Balcombe – merge into one another, mostly privately owned but with many footpaths. Hammer ponds, a relic of the once extensive iron industry, are numerous. North of the forest lie Crawley, a rapidly expanding new town, and

A cottage in the Forest Ridge, near Lower Beeding.

London's second airport at Gatwick, both of which are eating into Sussex.

The woodlands continue east, with the land steadily rising and becoming very broken with splendid views. Wakehurst Place, amongst the forest, has large tracts of typical Wealden woodland, in addition to its worldwide collection of trees and shrubs. Further east, beyond East Grinstead lies Ashdown Forest, now more heathland than forest. Early clearance of the forest allowed the rain to leach away the nutrients from this light sandy soil. It is now mainly an area of heather and bracken and rough pasture. Commoners have had rights in the forest since Norman times and, although much reduced, 6400 acres (2560 hectares) are still administered by the Board of Conservators. William Cobbett described it as 'verily the most villainously ugly spot I ever saw in England', but it is doubtful if the thousands of visitors who use the forest each year would agree with this. It is a very popular place in summer but can still be quiet and peaceful away from the main roads.

On the eastern edge of the Forest Ridge the Victorian creation of Crowborough has spilled over Beacon Hill, which at 792 feet (240 metres) is the highest point in the forest and higher than much of the Downs.

The Southern Forest Ridge

East and south of Ashdown Forest, the open character of the country changes to one of small meadows and rounded hills, and a series of long sandstone ridges and deep valleys. Many of these hills and ridges are as high as the main Forest Ridge and, although they are not as wild, the remoteness remains. The broken countryside stretches eastward along the Kent border and breaks into several ridges running south and east, which come to an abrupt halt in the cliffs at Hastings and the high ground at Rye and Winchelsea.

This is a delightful area of steep-sided val-

The Southern Forest Ridges near Burwash.

leys, ghylls, narrow lanes and excellent views. The eastern part of the county is deeply incised by the rivers Brede, Tillingham and Rother, which form wide valleys near the eastern border with Romney Marsh in Kent. This is a country of small arable farms and dairy and sheep farming. Hops are grown in places, although not as extensively as in the past, and the characteristic oasthouses, more popularly associated with Kent, are frequently seen.

Along the coast lie the modern resorts of Bexhill and St Leonards, which merge into the more historic Hastings. From here sandstone cliffs stretch along the coast, known as the Fire Hills from the colour of the gorse in winter; this is an enchanting place with steep wooded glens cutting into the cliffs and running down to the sea. The whole area is now protected as Fairlight Country Park. Beyond the cliffs lie Fairlight and then the long expanse of shingle beach known as Pett Level. The sea constantly removes shingle from this beach and deposits it further east at Rye Harbour, where it has built up so much that the once coastal towns of Rye and Winchelsea now lie 2 miles (3 km) inland. Rye still has its river entrance to the sea and by constant dredging remains a viable port. The dredged shingle is redeposited on Pett Level, which helps to protect the low-lying land behind. The shingle levels at Rye Harbour are an important breeding ground for seabirds and the area is now a nature reserve.

East of the river Rother lies the superb expanse of Camber Sands, backed by extensive sand dunes and extending to the Kent border. This is an excellent place for children, with safe bathing and perfect beaches.

The Low Weald

From the coast between Eastbourne and Bexhill the Low Weald extends north-west across the county. Many places are not much above sea level and from this area the Downs appear much higher. This is heavy land, nearly all clay, with occasional stretches of alluvium and sand and it is difficult to cultivate. In spring the land is cold and heavy and it may be difficult to break down the wet clods, whilst in dry weather it parches and cracks easily. The clay soil is, however, particularly suited to oaks and in places marvellous specimens can be found which may well be descendants of the great forest of Anderida. An area of woodland near Wisborough Green, known as The Mens, gives a glimpse of the old Weald.

A network of narrow lanes intersects the area and these are the best way to see the country, but not if you are in a hurry! Along the routes of the meandering rivers Adur and Arun, water-meadows give a distinctive air to the scenery and are reminiscent of Suffolk or Shropshire. These flat river lands, popular with anglers, flood in winter into long lakes alive with ducks and waterfowl.

There are only two towns of any size in the Low Weald, Haywards Heath and Burgess Hill, but there are numerous small towns and villages, such as Hailsham, Ringmer, Wisborough Green and Pulborough.

Along the coast little development has taken place, for the coastline here has changed dramatically over the last few centuries. When William of Normandy landed his fleet here in 1066, it was on the shore of a wide sea inlet which extended far inland. Pevensey, and the Roman fort of *Anderida*, were once lapped by the sea but are now 2 miles (3 km) inland. Silting of the estuary and subsequent draining of the marshland have created new farmland but the low-lying nature of the land and its susceptibility to flooding have discouraged development of the coast at this point. Only the small hamlets of Pevensey Bay and Normans Bay have sprung up to exploit the shingle beaches.

Building materials

Until the arrival of the railways, which provided cheap and convenient transport, buildings were constructed of the locally available materials. Some of the richer religious foundations used imported materials, but even here it was usually only in small features.

In the Weald the building material was oak; timber-framed buildings became highly sophisticated in their craftsmanship and reached their pinnacle in the 'Wealden hall-house'. This type of house is common throughout the Weald and Great Dixter, Northiam, and the Old Clergy House, Alfriston, are examples of hall-houses in more or less their original form.

Strawberry Hill Farm near Northiam: a good example of close timbering.

Over the centuries many timber-framed houses were altered externally by the application of tiles or weatherboard cladding or, in some cases, brick or stucco. Much of this was done to make the buildings more weather-proof but in the eighteenth century a form of tile-hanging was designed purely for fashionable reasons; this was the 'mathematical tile', which when applied resembled brick. Examples of these occur in many places, but particularly in Lewes.

Geological considerations also determined the pattern of building; in the downland and coastal regions from Eastbourne westwards, flint was extensively used. As with timber-framed buildings, this was also sometimes covered with stucco or tile-hanging, particularly in fashionable towns such as Brighton. North of the Downs a narrow belt of villages on the Upper Greensand ridge used this rough sandstone. Rather more widely used was a hard sandstone from the Hythe Beds a few miles further north. The villages around Midhurst and Petworth are particularly rich in this stone, which was usually named after the local quarry, such as Pulborough Stone. Near Petworth a form of limestone was quarried which consisted of massed fossilised shells of a freshwater snail. When polished it takes on a greenish-grey lustre and is known as Sussex marble or 'winkle-stone'.

From Tudor times brick started to be widely used for domestic buildings; the variety of clays resulted in an equal variety of colours, many of them very local in distribution. With the coming of the railways in the mid nineteenth century purely local materials diminished in use. Bricks could be more economically brought from the large factories in the Midlands and the small local brickworks gradually disappeared, although a handful struggled on until the Second World War and one or two small ones still survive.

History

Standing on some quiet part of the Downs or in woodland in the Weald, one can easily imagine that this is the landscape that early man knew. However, few landscapes in Britain are entirely natural and in Sussex man has had a particularly profound effect on the landscape.

Evidence of settlement in Sussex dates from about 3500 BC, when neolithic peoples landed in the south-east and pushed westwards along the Downs. They possessed the basic crafts of civilisation, such as pottery and agriculture, and had a highly organised social life. They built causewayed enclosures on the Downs and flint mining also took place; some two hundred mines have been identified at Cissbury.

The bronze age commenced about 2000 BC with the introduction of metal and new pottery types. There was also a change in climate to drier, colder weather and the population spread into the more hospitable Weald. Burial customs changed too, and the long barrows of neolithic times gave way to round barrows, which survive in large numbers. Between 600 and 400 BC flint and bronze gave way to iron, and farming was concentrated more on crops than on herding. New areas of the Weald were opened up and iron smelting started, mainly in the north-east of the county. Large hilltop enclosures were built, with impressive earthworks, as at Cissbury and Mount Caburn.

By the time of the Roman occupation in AD 43, Sussex to the west of Brighton was the main area of population, whilst to the east the population was mainly confined to the ironworking areas. There was rapid development and an increase in prosperity during the Roman occupation; the remains of nearly forty villas have been found, some very substantial as at Bignor and Fishbourne. *Noviomagus Regnensium* (Chichester) grew into a prosperous regional centre. The iron industry was expanded and the provision of good roads, such as Stane Street, simplified travel. There was also close contact between Sussex and the other parts of the Roman Empire.

Early in the fourth century nine Saxon Shore forts including *Anderida* (Pevensey) were built along the south coast as defences against Saxon raiders but from about AD 400 Roman garrisons were withdrawn to defend other parts of the Empire and successive raids led to the abandonment of villas and towns. In 477 the first record of the invasions appears in the Anglo-Saxon Chronicles and it took

The village pond at East Dean in West Sussex.

thirteen years for the Saxons to extend their control east to Pevensey, to establish the kingdom of the South Saxons. The area east of Pevensey, beyond the marshes, was occupied by a separate Saxon group, the Haestingas.

Sussex was now completely isolated from the rest of England. The existing populations were driven from their settlements; roads were abandoned and the dense forests became an effective barrier. The Saxons preferred small compact communities sharing great open fields. There is little evidence that they occupied existing towns or villages; most place-names now are Saxon and only a few Roman words persist. By 681, when St Wilfrid landed at Selsey, the landscape would have been very different from that which the Romans knew.

With the coming of Christianity a new period of peace and prosperity began and several of the old Roman towns re-emerged. By the tenth century mints were recorded in Lewes, Chichester and Hastings, a sign of an increasingly urban economy. A relatively brief period of insecurity occurred with the attacks by Viking raiders, which continued until 1016, when the Saxon Witan chose the Dane, Canute, as their king. A Saxon renais-

sance started and in the fifty years before the Norman invasion most of the surviving Saxon churches were built. One of these is at Bosham, which is depicted in the Bayeux Tapestry. It was here that Harold prayed before sailing to Normandy in 1064 to tell William that he was heir to the throne of England. When, on the death of Edward the Confessor, Harold accepted the throne for himself he set in motion a series of events which culminated in the battle of Hastings. William sailed with his invasion fleet, and on 14th October 1066 the two armies met at the site of the present town of Battle.

The Norman victory was absolute and resulted in a change in the laws, language and architecture of England. Sussex now became an important part of the country and, for a time, controlled communications with Normandy. The county was divided, north to south, into six administrative divisions called Rapes, based on Chichester, Arundel, Bramber, Lewes, Pevensey and Hastings, each given to one of William's most trusted barons.

A new period of expansion started; churches were built or rebuilt; abbeys and priories were started and ports such as Hastings, Rye and Shoreham grew in importance. By the fourteenth century, however, the harbours, which were so important for trade, were suffering badly from silting and erosion and the centre of trade moved eastward to Kent; Sussex once more declined.

In the late fifteenth century a new source of prosperity arrived; iron had been smelted since before the Romans, but the process was slow and inefficient. From northern France came the invention of the blast-furnace, which could produce twenty to thirty times the output of the old bloomeries. Sussex was well placed to exploit the new technology, as it had easily obtainable iron ore and an apparently limitless supply of timber. Streams were dammed to create 'hammer ponds' which provided a head of water to drive the hammers and bellows. The foundries produced many domestic products, but in particular armaments, both for home and export. Sir Walter Raleigh complained that English ships were being outgunned by foreign vessels armed with Sussex cannon, an early example of the arms trade! So important was the manufacture of arms that, during the Civil War, Parliamentary forces acted quickly to secure the county.

Iron brought great prosperity to Sussex but at a cost; the great Wealden forest was felled at an alarming rate. Royal commissions were appointed to investigate the problem and various regulations imposed, but with little effect. In the event it was technology which halted the deafforestation and industrialisation of Sussex. In the eighteenth century a process of smelting using coal was perfected and, with the iron ore having to be mined at deeper levels, the focus of ironworking moved to the Midlands. By 1720 only twenty forges remained working; the industry limped along until the last forge closed at Ashburnham in 1809. Sussex now returned to a rural economy, which it has largely retained to the present.

In the nineteenth century one area of expansion was the seaside resort. Following the popularisation of sea bathing as a medical treatment, most of the coastal towns began to expand. The coming of the railways helped this development, which has continued to the present.

In common with other south-eastern counties, Sussex has had to cope with a large increase in population since the First World War. Much of the development has taken place along the coast and uncontrolled development during the 1920s has resulted in an almost unbroken subtopia between Worthing and Peacehaven. Inland there has been a great deal of building along the northern borders. Strict planning regulations over the last few decades have attempted to strike a balance between the pressures of population and preserving that which is best in the county. Some of the beneficial effects of this planning were undone in the late 1980s when government policy changed, to give developers greater freedom. Many communities experienced rapid development over very short periods. There was much building of 'executive dwellings', upsetting the balance needed to provide affordable housing for young people, many of whom were forced to leave their villages. A further consequence was the failure of some developers to keep materials in character. Roads, too, have added to the pressures. Many towns and villages have benefited from by-passes and improved roads but roads have to go somewhere and there has often been a price to pay in the countryside. Once again it is a question of balance, but perhaps the major criticism is of the spate of ancillary development that takes place alongside new roads – shopping precincts and such like.

The balance seems to have swung back again now, at least as far as housing development is concerned, and there has been increasing use of planning powers to designate conservation areas. Parts of the South Downs and areas of the Weald have been declared 'Conservation Areas of Outstanding Landscape Value' and there are moves to have the Downs formed into a National Park. It is to be hoped that these and other measures will help to preserve in Sussex the richness and variety of its scenery and buildings.

2
Towns and villages

Alfriston

It is easy to see why Alfriston is so popular with visitors. Delightfully situated at the foot of the Downs in the gap cut by the Cuckmere river, the one main street is a picturesque jumble of timber-framed and tile-hung buildings; one of the best is the Star Inn, which dates from the fifteenth century and has some attractive carvings on the first-floor timbers. Outside the inn sits a large red-painted wooden lion, said to be the figurehead of a vessel wrecked on the nearby coast in the seventeenth century. The village is on the route of the South Downs Way and there are numerous pubs and tea rooms offering refreshments.

Behind the main street, and closer to the river, are the village green called the Tye and the large parish church of St Andrew, which dates from about 1360. A short distance away is the fourteenth-century Old Clergy House. Legend has it that the site for the church was chosen when four oxen hauling building materials lay down on the site, with their rumps touching, in the shape of a cross. A custom in Sussex was to bury shepherds with a tuft of wool in their hand, to explain to St Peter why they had not always attended church. The last known record of this custom is said to be at Alfriston in 1932.

A mile south of the village, where the road to Seaford crosses the crest of the Downs, is a viewpoint called High-and-Over, from which there are spectacular views over the Cuckmere valley and out to the Seven Sisters.

Old Clergy House, page 88; **South Downs Way**, page 62.

In the locality: Abbot's Wood Nature Reserve, page 57; Berwick church, page 76; Charleston Farmhouse, page 83; Coombe Hill, page 65; Drusillas, page 111; English Wine Centre, page 114; Friston Forest, page 61; Hunter's Burgh, page 66; Lullington church, page 80; Long Man of Wilmington, *page 66; Seven Sisters Country Park, page 62.*

Amberley

With its thatched roofs and brick and flint walls, this is one of the most picturesque villages in Sussex and much visited by artists and photographers. The village is laid out in a rough square with the church and castle at the north-west corner; by the church a track descends steeply, past the imposing curtain wall of the castle, to the water-meadows of the river Arun, known locally as the Wild Brooks.

The history of the settlement dates back to AD 670, when King Cadwalla granted lands to Bishop Wilfrid, but the present church of St Michael dates from about 1100. Inside there is a fourteenth-century chancel arch with some fine carving and traces of wall paintings. In the north wall there is a stained glass window in memory of Edward Stott, the nineteenth-century artist (died 1918), who lived in the village and is buried in the churchyard. Also buried in the churchyard is Arthur Rackham (1867–1939), best-known for his illustrations of children's books, including *Peter Pan.*

The Wild Brooks were partially drained some years ago but still provide fine wintering grounds for ducks and geese and other waterfowl. In the past flooding was so common that Amberley people were said to have webbed feet.

Amberley Castle, page 68; **Amberley Chalk Pits Museum**, page 95.

Arundel

Early closing Wednesday.

Built on the southern slopes of the Downs above the river Arun and dominated by its castle and 'Gothic' cathedral, this very picturesque market town has more the air of a town in northern France than of one in south-

Arundel High Street is one of the steepest in the country.

ern England. From the bridge over the Arun, the High Street, said to be the steepest in England, contains a collection of picturesque shops and inns huddled around the walls of the castle. Beside the bridge are the remains of the Blackfriars monastery dissolved in 1546 by Henry VIII.

The parish church dates from the fourteenth century and is unusual in that part of it, the Fitzalan Chapel, is reserved for Roman Catholic services. In the nineteenth century, following a legal dispute, the chapel was declared the private property of the Dukes of Norfolk and a wall was built to separate the chapel from the rest of the church. The wall has been replaced by a glass and wrought-iron screen but the chapel can be entered only from the castle grounds. There are some interesting brasses and monuments in the church.

The Roman Catholic cathedral was built in 1870 in the French Gothic style of 1300 by J. A. Hansom and Son, who also invented the hansom cab. Some would say that the latter was their better work, but the effect is impres-sive, particularly when seen with the castle from a distance.

Arundel Museum and Heritage Centre, page 95; **Arundel Castle,** page 68; **Arundel Toy and Military Museum,** page 95; **Wildfowl and Wetlands Trust,** page 110.

In the locality: Amberley Chalk Pits Museum, page 95; Arundel Vineyard, page 113; Bignor Roman Villa, page 65; Boxgrove Priory, page 73; Burpham church, page 76; Climping church, page 78; Climping Beach, page 63; Fairmile Bottom, page 60; Ford church, page 79; Hardham church, page 79; Halnaker Windmill, page 107; Highdown Hill, page 66; Highdown Gardens, page 86; Parham House, page 89; Pulborough Brooks RSPB Reserve, page 62; Slindon Estate, page 62.

Ashburnham
Ashburnham Furnace, page 105; Church of St Peter, page 75.

Ashurst
Church of St James, page 76.

Battle

Early closing Wednesday; market days Friday and Saturday.

On 14th October 1066 there took place on this site the most momentous battle ever to be fought on English soil. This became known as the battle of Hastings and the Norman victory was to bring about a complete change in the laws, architecture and society of England. On the site of his victory William had an abbey built and this attractive little market town has grown up around it. At first the townspeople worshipped in the abbey church but in the twelfth century a parish church was built opposite the abbey walls. There are some interesting monuments and brasses in the church.

In front of the abbey gatehouse the old market place is now used as a car park but in November there are bonfire celebrations here which rival those at Lewes. On one corner of the market place are the Pilgrim's Rest tearooms, a very attractive timber-framed house dating from the fifteenth century.

The short High Street runs north from the abbey and is a pleasant collection of shops and inns, some incorporating stone from Battle Abbey. At the north end of the town, near the present market place, the offices of Rother District Council are housed on a site known as Watch Oak. Local legend has it that from this point, from the branches of an ancient oak tree which stood until recently, King Harold's mistress, Edith of the Swan Neck, watched the fateful battle.

There is a very attractive windmill on the outskirts of the town.

Battle Abbey, page 73; **Buckleys Yesterday's World**, page 95; **Museum of Local History**, page 95; **Town Model**, page 95.

In the locality: Ashburnham church, page 75; Ashburnham Furnace, page 105; Bateman's, page 83; Bodiam Castle, page 68; Brickwall House, page 83; Carr Taylor Vineyard, page 113; Footlands Wood, page 60; Fore Wood, page 61; Great Dixter, page 85; Herstmonceux Castle, page 70; Herstmonceux church, page 79; Leeford Vineyard, page 114; Ninfield stocks, page 108; Penhurst church, page 80; Quarry Farm Rural Experience, page 112; Sedlescombe Vineyard, page 114; Thomas Smith's Trug Shop, page 113.

Berwick

Church, page 76.

Bexhill-on-Sea

Early closing Wednesday.

This pleasantly laid-out seaside resort is one of the later developments on the Sussex coast and is especially attractive to those who seek more genteel pastimes than those provided by other resorts. This, together with an equable climate, has made Bexhill very popular as a retirement area. The seafront is dominated by the De La Warr Pavilion, now a Grade 1 listed building, designed by Eric Mendelsohn and Serge Chermayeff of the Bauhaus School of Design in 1936. Very avant-garde in its time, and a tribute to the adventurousness of the then town councillors, it seems ordinary now, a reflection of how acceptable the influence of the designers has become.

The old town of Bexhill lies half a mile (800 metres) inland from the sea and was built on land granted by Offa, king of Mercia, for a church in 772. Not much remains of the old town but there are some attractive weatherboarded houses clustered around the church. The church itself was built in the twelfth century but was heavily restored in 1878; on the inside wall of the tower is a carved coffin slab from the grave of a Saxon child which was found under the nave during the restoration.

Off the beach to the east of the town, below Galley Hill, the tree stumps of a petrified forest can be seen at very low tides and there is much evidence of dinosaurs in the area, some of it on display in the local museum.

Bexhill Museum, page 97; **Museum of Costume and Social History**, page 97.

In the locality: Ashburnham church, page 75; Ashburnham Furnace, page 105; Battle Abbey, page 73; Footlands Wood, page 60; Fore Wood, page 61; Herstmonceux Castle, page 70; Herstmonceux church, page 79; Penhurst church, page 80; Pevensey Castle, page 67; Thomas Smith's Trug Shop, page 113.

Bignor
Roman Villa, page 65.

Billingshurst
Early closing Wednesday.
This large village has grown up along the A29 London to Bognor Regis road, which is part of the Roman road Stane Street.

The parish church, which dates from the thirteenth century, has been heavily over-restored but there is an attractive fifteenth-century wagon roof with over 120 carved bosses at the intersections. Near the church is a pretty collection of cottages and opposite is a sixteenth-century half-timbered inn, Ye Olde Six Bells. A little further away is the Unitarian church, which dates from 1754 and is an agreeable cottage-like building.

In the locality: Amberley Chalk Pits Museum, page 95; Bignor Roman Villa, page 65; Blue Idol Meeting House, page 76; Coultershaw Water Pump, page 106; Hardham church, page 79; Hollygate Cactus Nursery, page 112; King's Mill, page 108; Nutbourne Vineyard, page 114; Parham House, page 89; Petworth House, page 90; Pulborough Brooks RSPB Reserve, page 62; Shipley Hammer Pond, page 109; The Mens, page 61.

Bishopstone
Church of St Andrew, page 76.

Bodiam
Bodiam Castle, page 68; Bodiam Ferry Company, page 110; Quarry Farm Rural Experience, page 112.

Bognor Regis
Early closing Wednesday.
This agreeable seaside resort at the eastern end of the Selsey peninsula is renowned for its excellent sandy beaches and its equable climate. Bognor was one of the earliest seaside resorts to be developed, having been started in the 1780s by Sir Richard Hotham MP, who began an ambitious scheme for Bognor to rival Brighton and Bath as a fashionable town. As with his plans to change the name to Hothampton, he never quite succeeded. Sir Richard's own house, built in 1792 and now owned by the corporation, is considered to be the best Georgian house in Sussex.

Bognor achieved a limited success in its plans to become 'the resort of more select company', as a nineteenth-century guide put it; Queen Victoria called it her 'dear little Bognor' and it was the setting for Jane Austen's *Sanditon*. Despite the much quoted dying epithet of George V, Bognor was a favourite spot for the king and in 1929, after he had spent a period of convalescence here, he bestowed the title 'Regis' on it.

All the usual attractions of the seaside resort can be found in Bognor, including a pier from which competitors in the annual International Birdman Competition try to defy gravity. Perhaps not surprisingly, the town is also host to the European Clowns' Convention.

Bognor Regis Local History Museum, page 97; **Butlin's South Coast World**, page 110.

In the locality: Boxgrove Priory, page 73; Chichester Harbour, page 59; Climping Beach, page 63; Climping church, page 78; Denmans, page 84; Fishbourne Roman Villa, page 65; Goodwood House, page 85; Goodwood Country Park, page 61; Halnaker Mill, page 107; Pagham Harbour, page 76; Slindon Park, page 62; Tangmere Museum of Aviation, page 104; The Trundle, page 67; Weald and Downland Museum, page 104.

Bosham
Pronounced 'Bozzum' by the locals, this is one of the truly delightful villages of Sussex. Situated on a narrow inlet of Chichester Harbour and with a close-packed huddle of cottages around the waterfront green and church, Bosham is very charming indeed.

The small quay and the waters of Chichester Harbour are a constant source of attraction, with small craft busily coming and going and a good variety of seabirds. The village green is in the care of the National Trust, which should ensure that the waterside scene is safe from development. Apart from its scenic attractions, Bosham is an historic site. It is believed that the Roman emperor Vespasian had a residence here in AD 69–

The waterfront at Bosham on Chichester Harbour.

79 and that at a later date this was the spot at which King Canute demonstrated the fallibility of royalty by his inability to command the waves.

The church, which is probably built over the site of a Roman basilica, may have been founded by Canute himself. Although this is unproven, local legend said that Canute's eight-year-old daughter was buried in the church and when the site was excavated in 1865 an eleventh-century coffin was found which contained the bones of an eight-year-old child. What is beyond doubt is that Bosham was the home and place of worship of Earl Godwin and his son Harold, who later became King Harold and was defeated at the battle of Hastings in 1066. In the Bayeux Tapestry, Harold is shown praying in Bosham church before setting sail for Normandy in 1064 to see William. A further excavation in 1965 revealed another coffin, which is believed to contain the remains of Earl Godwin. Although there have been many additions to the church, there is much of the Saxon work in evidence including the tower.

Another attraction is Bosham Walk, a small arcade of craft and gift shops, which has been created from a series of old cottages.

In the locality: Fishbourne Roman Villa, page 65; Kingley Vale, page 61; Stansted House, page 92.

Boxgrove
Boxgrove Priory, page 73.

Bramber
Bramber Castle and Church, page 69; St Mary's, page 91.

Brightling
This small village consists of a church and a few houses and little else except delightful surroundings. The church dates from the thirteenth century and inside there are remnants of fourteenth-century wall paintings.

Over the churchyard wall can be seen Brightling Park, once the home of 'Mad' Jack Fuller, a local squire and eccentric who sat as member of Parliament for Sussex from 1801 to 1812 after allegedly spending £50,000 to secure his election. To provide work for the local people, he had a wall built around his estate, much of which still stands, along with a number of follies. One of these, Brightling Needle, is a short distance away on Brightling Down, which, at 646 feet (213 metres) above sea level, gives tremendous views and was one of the Armada beacon sites. Nearby is the observatory built by Fuller and painted several times by the artist Turner.

In the churchyard is Fuller's mausoleum, a large pyramid, which he had built in 1810 and in which he intended to be buried. The house opposite was once the local inn, but the vicar disliked the competition and in return for allowing Fuller to build the mausoleum he made him close the inn and build a new one about a mile away. This still flourishes as the Fuller's Arms. However, despite local legend which holds that Fuller is interred in the pyramid, sitting up and holding a bottle of port, it seems his wishes were not observed because when the tomb was opened in 1982 it was found to be empty – a pity!

In the locality: Ashburnham church, page 75; Ashburnham Furnace, page 105; Bateman's, page 83; Penhurst church, page 80.

Brighton

Early closing Wednesday and Thursday.
Brighton and Hove form the largest metropolitan area in Sussex and the best-known seaside resort in southern England.

Brighton had been mentioned in Domesday Book and was a fairly substantial fishing village called Brighthelmstone. Successive French raids in the fourteenth century encouraged the residents to place a wall around the town but the depredations of the sea had by the mid eighteenth century engulfed part of the old town and it was a place of little importance. In 1753 Dr Russell of Lewes published his treatise on the use of sea water and its curative properties and, having also discovered a chalybeate spring in the town, encouraged his patients to visit Brighthelmstone. The doctor set up house in what became the Royal Albion Hotel and the visitors started to arrive at this, the first of the seaside resorts. The final seal of approval was the patronage of the Prince Regent, who, after secretly marrying Mrs Fitzherbert, took up residence here in a farmhouse which was later remodelled into the Royal Pavilion. The insignificant fishing village now became a fashionable town called Brighton and development of the attractive Regency terraces and crescents started

as early as 1780. Much of the building, however, took place in the 1820s when an improved coach road made the town more accessible, fast coaches taking under six hours for the journey from London. The coming of the railways in the 1850s brought the town within reach of ordinary people. Thousands of people settled in the town and many thousands more flocked in to enjoy the delights of the seaside.

With the visitors came the expansion of the attractions and Brighton has been described as 'a mixture of the raucous and the refined'. Along the 4 miles (6 km) of seafront are all the usual facilities, including two piers (although one is now in a sad state of repair) and the many other delights of a seaside resort. Added to all this is the naturally attractive setting on the southern slopes of the Downs.

Brighton is more than a seaside resort, however; it has excellent shopping facilities, good theatres and museums and an active arts and concert programme.

Although physically part of Brighton, **Hove** is administratively separate and has an identity of its own. The development of the old fishing village of Hove started some fifty years after Brighton and therefore missed the golden age of Regency architecture. However, there are some attractive buildings around open spaces and gardens and Hove presents a quieter atmosphere than its brasher neighbour.

Town walk
This walk traces the development of Brighton from fishing village to fashionable resort. The old town was bounded by East, West and North Streets and the seafront, which replaces the original South Street. Little remains of buildings before the eighteenth century, but the area is still based on the layout of the old medieval village and contains the area known as the Lanes. This is a delightful area of antique, bric-a-brac and book shops and contains some good restaurants and pubs.

Start at the Old Ship Hotel on the seafront, the oldest pub in Brighton. The front is nineteenth-century but behind lie the Assembly Rooms dating from 1767. Go along Ship

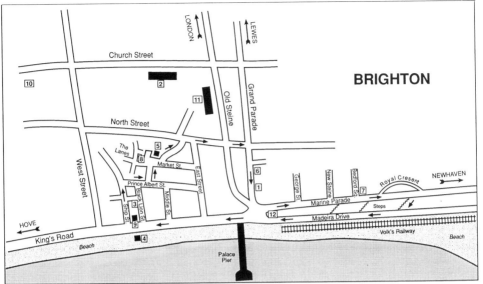

Brighton street plan: 1 Birthplace of Sir Edward Marshall Hall; 2 Brighton Museum and Art Gallery; 3 Cricketers' Arms; 4 Fisherman's Museum; 5 House of Correction; 6 House of Dr Gideon Mantell; 7 House of Terence Rattigan; 8 Old Pump House; 9 Old Ship Hotel; 10 Parish Church; 11 Royal Pavilion; 12 Sea Life Centre.

Lane, which contains some good bow-fronted houses and also some faced with knapped flint. On the corner of Prince Albert Street, on the left, the antique shop shows a good use of cobbles in its construction.

Turn right, and follow Prince Albert Street around. Off to the right, in Black Lion Street, is the Cricketers' Arms, an eighteenth-century coaching inn. Next to it is Black Lion Lane, one of many very narrow thoroughfares which are probably medieval in origin. Turn left to Market Place and on the left the Old Pump House is a good example of the use of black mathematical tiles. Opposite is the original House of Correction, built in 1835. In the corner of the square, Meeting House Lane is a particularly attractive twitten with some jettied houses in it. Follow the lane around to the right and explore the lanes and twittens before returning to Market Street. Then, take the lane to the right of the House of Correction through into North Street, the boundary of the old town but now a modern shopping street. The parish church lies about half a

mile (800 metres) inland, well away from the old town.

Across North Street is the Royal Pavilion, the start of fashionable Brighton, and to the right is the Old Steine, which runs northwards from the seafront and past the front of the Pavilion. Now laid out as formal gardens intersected by busy roads, this was originally common land where the fishermen laid their nets to dry beside a small stream.

The next stage of development was east of the Steine, so cross the road carefully, past the impressive fountain with entwined dolphins built in the early 1800s, and turn right towards the sea. There are some attractive Regency houses on this side with wrought-iron canopied balconies. Just past Steine Street, Number 20 is the house of Dr Gideon Mantell (1790–1852), who discovered *Iguanodon*, and a little further along is the birthplace of the lawyer Sir Edward Marshall Hall (1858–1927). Turn left at the seafront along Marine Parade. The immediate area here is one of the 'less refined' parts but

Royal Crescent, Brighton.

further along Marine Parade there are many attractive Regency houses and behind the seafront lies an attractive Regency town with fine terraces, especially in the roads running north from the seafront.

George Street contains a fine group of bow-fronted houses and the New Steine, built about 1810, is a pleasant development of terraced houses along either side of formal gardens. Rock Place has some small cottages which appear to be older than the surrounding Regency buildings.

On the corner of Bedford Square, a pleasant town house was once the home of Terence Rattigan (1911–77), the playwright, and then a very fine terrace of bow-fronted houses with canopied balconies leads to Royal Crescent, started in 1798, a little before the surrounding development. This is a most attractive shallow crescent, faced with black mathematical tiles, and all the houses have canopied balconies. Development of Kemp Town continued eastward with some attractive terraces and squares, but cross the road and descend the steps to sea level and return to the Palace Pier along Madeira Drive.

Alongside the beach runs the Volk's Rail-

way and on the landward side a covered promenade with some fine wrought ironwork runs the whole length of Madeira Drive. Continue on past the pier to the starting point at Ship Lane. The next stage in development was westwards into Hove along a couple of miles of seafront and then development continued northwards to the Downs.

Booth Museum of Natural History, page 97; **Brighton Museum and Art Gallery,** page 97; **British Engineerium,** page 100; **Fisherman's Museum,** page 97; **Hove Museum and Art Gallery,** page 101; **Preston Manor,** page 97; **Regency Town House Tour,** page 112; **Royal Pavilion,** page 90; **Sea Life Centre,** page 110; **Sussex Toy and Model Museum,** page 98; **Volk's Railway,** page 109.

In the locality: Clayton church, page 78; Clayton windmills, page 106; Coombes Farm Tours, page 111; Danny, page 83; Devil's Dyke, page 65; Ditchling Beacon, page 60; Foredown Tower Countryside Centre, page 60; Newtimber Place, page 88; Rottingdean Grange, page 102; West Blatchington windmill, page 109; Wood's Mill Countryside Centre, page 63.

Broadwater

See under Worthing, page 56.

Burgess Hill

Early closing Wednesday.

This flourishing modern residential town has grown up around a Victorian village which owed its existence to its position on the main London to Brighton railway.

The main street which runs from the station to the church has no buildings of special note but is an attractive shopping area.

In the past Burgess Hill was the site of an annual sheep fair of some importance.

In the locality: Clayton church, page 78; Clayton windmills, page 106; Danny, page 83; Ditchling Beacon, page 60; Ditchling Common Country Park, page 60; Rock Lodge vineyard, page 114; Twineham church, page 82.

Burpham

Church of St Mary the Virgin, page 76.

Burwash

With its extremely attractive High Street, this is one of the show villages of Sussex. White weatherboarding and tile-hung buildings predominate and brick footpaths and pollarded lime trees make for a neat and tidy appearance.

The village sits high on a ridge between the rivers Rother and Dudwell and there are some commanding views. The church has a Norman tower with a shingled spire and the nave and chancel are Early English but were rebuilt in 1856. The war memorial by the church was unveiled by Rudyard Kipling, who lived nearby at Bateman's, and whose son is one of those commemorated. It is unusual in that there is a light in the top which is lit on the birthday of each of those commemorated.

A short distance down the High Street is Rampyndene, the best building in the village. Built in 1699 by a timber merchant, it is timber-framed, although this is not obvious from the brick and tile-hung front.

Bateman's, page 83; **Bateman's watermill**, page 105.

In the locality: Etchingham church, page 78; Haremere Hall, page 86.

Bury

This very appealing village lies just off the A29 on the west bank of the river Arun. There was once a ferry across the river to Amberley on the east bank.

Much of the building is of local sandstone, but there is some flint, most noticeably in the church of St John, which is partly Norman but dates mostly from the thirteenth century.

John Galsworthy (1867–1933), the novelist, lived and died in the village at Bury House, a Tudor-style building dating from 1910. Next door to it is the nineteenth-century post office with some unusual carvings on the exterior.

In the locality: Amberley Chalk Pits Museum, page 95; Bignor Roman Villa, page 65.

Cade Street

See under Heathfield, page 35.

Chichester

Early closing Thursday; market day Wednesday.

The administrative capital of West Sussex and the cathedral city of Sussex, Chichester traces its origins back to the first century BC, when Belgae invaders built their town of *Noviomagus* near the head of the navigable harbour. A century later the Romans occupied the city, renamed it *Regnum*, built walls around it, which can still be traced in parts, and laid out the grid pattern of streets which still forms the basis of the city plan. In many places it is possible to walk along sections of the medieval town walls, which still follow the line of the Roman walls.

The Romans also built the main road to London which the Saxons later called Stane Street. Many Roman remains have been discovered in and around the city.

With the coming of the Saxons in the fifth century, the city was renamed Cissa's Caestra, or camp, and was one of the few Roman sites that the Saxons occupied in Sussex. It was not, however, until the Norman rationalisation of sees that the bishopric moved from nearby Selsey to Chichester.

Although based on the Roman plan, Chichester is mainly a Georgian city, but there are also many medieval buildings. Brick has been very attractively used, and also flint, which, with its closeness to the Downs, is the local stone.

The four main streets, named from the points of the compass, radiate from the market cross, which is built of Caen stone and was given to the city by Bishop Edward Story in 1501. The elaborately carved octagonal structure was regularly damaged by traffic until 1976, when a pedestrian precinct was established around it.

Chichester is a compact and attractive city and in close contact with its cathedral, which is unusual in that the cathedral close is not cut off from the city. It has been able to avoid, so far, the problems of urban sprawl associated with many cities. Situated on the Coastal Plain with the South Downs forming a backdrop, it has the added advantage of attractive surrounding countryside and the nearby Chichester Harbour. A 6 mile (10 km) foot and cycle path to the harbour from the city has been created along the Chichester Canal. There are numerous museums and galleries, and the Chichester Festival Theatre, which opened in 1962 with Lord Olivier as its first director, ranks as one of England's leading theatres.

City walk

From the Market Cross head down South Street. In a short distance, on the right, is the Vicar's Hall and Crypt dating from the thirteenth century. Now a restaurant, it was probably originally a guildhall for the local merchants. Opposite is the timber-framed White Horse inn, dating from 1416 and an inn from at least the early seventeenth century.

Turn left into West Pallant; immediately ahead is the thirteenth-century former church of All Saints, now used as a Red Cross centre. The Pallants is the best Georgian area in the city and so-called because it was once a palatinate of the Archbishops of Canterbury. The area is based around a central crossroads, each arm of which is again named after the points of the compass, and contains many fine buildings. The best of these is Pallant House at the crossroads. Built by Henry Peckham in 1720, it is now an art gallery.

It is worth exploring each of the roads

Georgian cottages in The Pallants, Chichester.

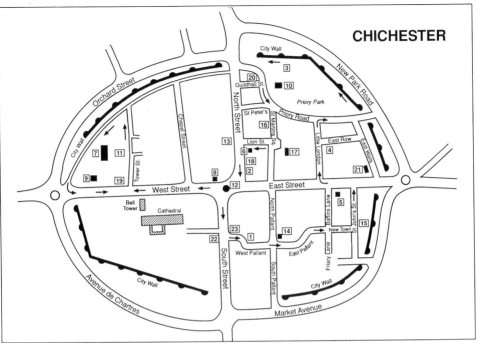

Chichester street plan: 1 All Saints' church; 2 Buttermarket; 3 Castle Mound; 4 Chichester District Museum; 5 Corn Exchange; 6 Council Chamber; 7 County Hall; 8 Dolphin and Anchor Hotel; 9 Edes House; 10 Guildhall Museum; 11 Library; 12 Market Cross; 13 Marks & Spencer; 14 Pallant House Gallery; 15 St John's church; 16 St Martin's; 17 St Mary's Hospital; 18 St Olave's church (SPCK); 19 St Peter's church; 20 Ship Hotel; 21 Shippams factory; 22 Vicar's Hall and Crypt; 23 White Horse inn.

making up the Pallants and then continuing along East Pallant past more fine Georgian houses and, on the corner of Baffins Lane, an attractive terrace of Georgian cottages. Continue to St John's Street and turn left. Opposite, the octagonal brick building is St John's church, built in 1812. Turn into East Street. Off to the right is the Shippams fish-paste factory, which was founded in the city in 1750; look for the giant wishbone hanging from the clock. To the left is the former Corn Exchange built in 1830 and now housing a Macdonalds hamburger house! Turn right into Little London, reputedly named by Queen Elizabeth I because its busyness reminded her of London, but in fact the name was in use about a century earlier. At the junction with East Row is the District Museum.

Cross Priory Road and in a short distance,

on the right, enter Priory Park and continue left along the top of the city walls. In the park the mound of the Norman motte and bailey castle can be seen and also the Guildhall, originally the chancel of the thirteenth-century Franciscan friary, now used as a museum. There are some fine trees in the park and splendid views of the city and cathedral from the walls.

Continue around the walls into Priory Lane and back to Priory Road. On the corner of Guildhall Street is the Ship Hotel, built in 1790 for Admiral Sir George Murray, one of Nelson's captains at the battle of Copenhagen. General Eisenhower stayed here on the eve of the D-Day landings in June 1944.

Cross Priory Road into St Martin's Square. On the left is a very fine five-bay Georgian house, Number 7, with a handsome arched doorway. There are a number of good cottages down here, especially St Martin's on the right, tiny, with an attractive clock above the door. Further along on the left are the almshouses of St Mary's Hospital, which moved to the site in 1253. The chapel and parts of the old buildings are open to visitors by appointment. The road widens here into a small square and there are some particularly attractive houses, some with Venetian windows. This is where the weekly hog market used to be held!

Take the narrow lane opposite St Mary's, Lion Street, into North Street. On the corner is the Council Chamber, in brick with a colonnaded front; it was built in 1731 by public subscription. Opposite, look above Marks & Spencer at the Venetian window. It is worth exploring North Street to the right before continuing left to the Market Cross.

Southwards, just past the Council Chamber,

In Chichester, the market cross stands at the intersection of the four main streets.

is St Olave's church, dating originally from 1050 but restored in 1850 and now an SPCK bookshop, and further along is the Buttermarket, built in 1807 to a design of John Nash.

Back at the Market Cross, turn right into West Street, past the very fine coaching inn, the Dolphin and Anchor Hotel, originally two separate inns, and on past the cathedral and into Tower Street. A short distance down on the left is the very striking circular public library built in 1967 and behind that County Hall. Continue down Tower Street, through a pleasant modern development, to the walls and continue left along the top of the wall past County Hall to West Street and back to the cathedral.

Shortly, on the left, is Edes House, one of the finest buildings in the city. Built by John Edes in 1696, it was at one time thought to have been by Sir Christopher Wren. It served for some years as the county hall until the new one was built in 1937.

Back at the cathedral, opposite the unique detached bell-tower, is St Peter's church, looking Gothic, but built in 1852. It is well worth exploring the cathedral and its precincts before completing the tour.

Cathedral, page 76; **Chichester District Museum**, page 98; **Guildhall Museum**, page 98; **Mechanical Music and Doll Museum**, page 98; **Pallant House Gallery**, page 98.

In the locality: Boxgrove Priory, page 73; Chichester Harbour, page 59; Chilsdown Vineyard, page 113; Denmans, page 84; Earnley Butterflies and Gardens, page 111; Goodwood Country Park, page 61; Goodwood House, page 85; Halnaker Windmill, page 107; Kingley Vale, page 61; North Marden church, page 80; Pagham Harbour, page 61; Slindon Estate, page 62; Stansted House, page 92; Tangmere Military Aviation Museum, page 104; The Trundle, page 67; Uppark, page 92; Weald and Downland Open Air Museum, page 104.

Clayton
Church of St John the Baptist, page 78; Clayton windmills, page 106.

Climping
Church of St Mary, page 78.

Crawley

Early closing Wednesday; market day Thursday.

This rapidly expanding new town was based on the old market town of Crawley on the main London to Brighton road. Designated a new town under the Act of 1946, it has expanded to incorporate the neighbouring villages of Ifield and Three Bridges. With its proximity to Gatwick Airport, and the expansion of that, it is certain that Crawley will continue to grow.

The High Street of old Crawley has been used as the spine of the new town and there are a number of attractive timber-framed houses and inns, the best of which is the George inn. The new shopping centre at Queen's Square has been built to one side of the High Street and is considered to be one of the best-planned shopping areas in the county. The residential areas have also employed up-to-date planning practices and are grouped in a series of 'neighbourhood units' centred on Queen's Square. The town also seems to have avoided the 1960s preoccupation with tower blocks.

Three Bridges has been entirely absorbed into the new town, but **Ifield** has managed to retain a certain amount of its village atmosphere and has a number of pretty buildings in its main street.

In the locality: High Beeches, page 86; Leonardslee Gardens, page 87; Mannings Heath hammer ponds, page 108; Nymans Garden, page 88; Priest's House, West Hoathly, page 90; Tilgate Park, page 63; Wakehurst Place, page 94; Worth church, page 82.

Crowborough

Early closing Wednesday.

A straggling place of suburban character, Crowborough takes its name from Crowborough Beacon, which at 792 feet (240 metres) is the highest point on the Forest Ridge and gives glorious views of Ashdown Forest. The town grew up from the sale of part of the forest in the eighteenth century but was much enlarged in the nineteenth.

Sir Arthur Conan Doyle (1859–1930) lived for some time at Crowborough, as did another writer, Richard Jefferies (1848–87). It was also the birthplace, in 1898, of Jack Russell Lambert, who, at 2 feet 10 inches (85 cm), was the smallest person born in England, being 6 inches (150 mm) shorter than the legendary Tom Thumb.

In the locality: Ashdown Forest, page 57; Barnsgate Manor Vineyard, page 113; Moorlands, page 87.

Ditchling

Ditchling Museum, page 98; Stoneywish Country Park, page 62.

In the locality: Clayton church, page 78; Devil's Dyke, page 65; Ditchling Beacon, page 60; Ditchling Common Country Park, page 60.

Eastbourne

Early closing Wednesday.

Few resorts can rival the elegance and grandeur of the 3 mile (5 km) seafront at Eastbourne, which extends eastwards to the slopes of Beachy Head. Justly called the 'Empress of Watering Places', Eastbourne is one of the more recent of Sussex seaside resorts. The main development was started in 1851 by the Dukes of Devonshire, whose family still owns much of the town, but the town did not receive its charter until 1883.

Along the elegant seafront not one shop has been allowed and the emphasis in entertainment is on the quiet and refined. There is, however, a pier, erected in 1888, which has all the amenities a good pier should have. In one of the houses on Marine Parade Charles Darwin wrote part of his *Origin of Species*.

Behind the front lie a good modern shopping area, some pleasant parks and a fine concert hall. One mile (1.6 km) inland lies the original village of Eastbourne. Now engulfed in the modern residential area, it retains a number of its old buildings. The church dates from about 1200 and opposite is the Lamb inn, which is a very fine timber-framed building.

Butterfly Centre, page 111; **Heritage Centre**, page 98; **'How We Lived Then' Museum of Shops**, page 99; **Martello Tower 73 (Wish Tower)**, page 72; **Museum of the Royal National Lifeboat Institution**, page

The seafront at Eastbourne.

99; **Redoubt Fortress,** page 72; **Towner Art Gallery and Local History Museum,** page 99.

In the locality: Beachy Head, page 58; Coombe Hill, page 65; Filching Manor Motor Museum, page 99; Friston Forest, page 61; Hunter's Burgh, page 66; Long Man of Wilmington, page 66; Michelham Priory, page 74; Old Clergy House, page 88; Pevensey Castle, page 67; Polegate Windmill, page 109; Seven Sisters Country Park, page 62; Seven Sisters Sheep Centre, page 112.

East Dean
(East Sussex)

There has been much expansion of this downland village, but mainly to the north of the coast road. The older centre to the south remains an attractive flint village grouped around a small green off the road to Birling Gap and the cliffs at Beachy Head, probably the most attractive stretch of coastline in the county. The delightful Tiger inn is the oldest secular building in the village and dates from the sixteenth century. The church of St Simon and St Jude dates in part from Norman times but has been much restored. There is a Tapsell gate into the churchyard. These gates turn on a

central pivot and are peculiar to Sussex.

Seven Sisters Sheep Centre, page 112.

In the locality: Beachy Head, page 58; Friston Forest, page 61; Seven Sisters Country Park, page 62; South Downs Way, page 62.

East Grinstead
Early closing Wednesday; market day Saturday.

This flourishing market town and rapidly expanding residential area on the edge of Ashdown Forest owes its expansion largely to its railway link with London. Although there is much modern development, it has retained the nucleus of its old town with its very attractive High Street. There are many interesting buildings, including Sackville College, a series of almshouses dating from 1609, and the very fine Dorset Arms, dating from the eighteenth century.

The church has suffered a number of misfortunes; the present building dates from 1789. In 1683 the tower was struck by lightning and the bells melted; in 1785 the tower collapsed; in 1836 a pinnacle was blown off and in 1930 another fell through the roof. Needless to say, there has been much restoration!

On the outskirts of the town is the Queen

Victoria Hospital, where Sir Archibald MacIndoe pioneered plastic surgery. **Sackville College**, page 90.

In the locality: Ashdown Forest, page 57; Borde Hill Garden, page 83; Hammerwood, page 86; Holtye Common Roman road, page 66; Kidbrooke Park, page 86; Priest's House, West Hoathly, page 90; Sheffield Park, page 91; Standen, page 91; Wakehurst Place, page 94.

Edburton
See under Poynings, page 43.

Etchingham
Church of St Mary and St Nicholas, page 78; Haremere Hall, page 86.

Fletching
This historic village is attractively situated in wooded countryside and has some good timber-framed houses in it. It was here that Simon de Montfort and his troops rested before the battle of Lewes in 1264 and de Montfort is said to have held a vigil in the church the night before the battle. Much restored, the church dates mainly from the thirteenth century but has a Norman tower and a number of interesting brasses, one of which is to a follower of Jack Cade's rebellion in 1450. Edward Gibbon (1737–94) is also buried in the church. He was a friend of the Sheffield family and a frequent visitor to their home at nearby Sheffield Park.

A short distance away lies the nondescript hamlet of **Piltdown**, which became famous in 1912 with the discovery of 'Piltdown Man', and infamous in the 1950s when this was found to be a fraud!

In the locality: Barnsgate Manor Vineyard, page 113; Bluebell Railway, page 106; Chailey Windmill, page 106; Sheffield Park, page 91.

Ford
Church of St Andrew, page 79.

Fulking
See under Poynings, page 43.

Glynde
Church of St Mary, page 79; Glynde Place, page 84.

Goring-by-Sea
See under Worthing, page 56.

Hailsham
Early closing Thursday; market day Wednesday.

Hailsham is a small market town which grew up around a railway line and continued to flourish even after the railway closed. The central residential part is mainly Victorian and there has been much modern development, but there are a few attractive Georgian buildings in the High Street and the church dates in part from the fifteenth century.

Besides being an agricultural town, Hailsham is noted for its ropemaking, which started in 1807. At one time it had the dubious honour of supplying all the rope for the public hangman.

In the locality: Abbot's Wood, page 57; Cuckoo Trail, page 59; Filching Manor Motor Museum, page 99; Herstmonceux Castle, page 70; Herstmonceux church, page 79; Thomas Smith's Trug Shop, page 113; Merrydown Wine Company, page 114; Michelham Priory, page 74; Pevensey Castle, page 67; Polegate Windmill, page 109.

Hardham
Church of St Botolph, page 79.

Hastings
Early closing Wednesday.

Famous for the great battle to which it gave its name, Hastings is now an attractive all-year resort. Sheltered by tall cliffs, it enjoys high sunshine and temperature figures and, as its postal cancellation stamp once said, has been popular with visitors since 1066!

After the Conquest William I made Hastings his headquarters and in the twelfth century it became chief of the Cinque Ports. However, with its constant problems of erosion and silting, it had already declined in importance by the thirteenth century. The great cliff on which William built his castle has fallen away, taking much of the castle with it, and of Hastings's original seven medieval churches only two remain, St Clement's and All Saints'. At the eastern end lies the Old Town and the harbour area, with the

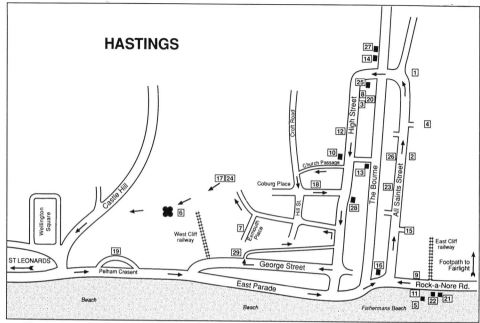

Hastings street plan: 1 All Saints' church; 2 All Saints' Cottage; 3 Apothecary House; 4 Ebenezer Chapel; 5 Fisherman's Museum; 6 Hastings Castle; 7 House of Elizabeth Blackwell; 8 House of Rossetti; 9 Mermaid; 10 Museum of Local History; 11 Net shops; 12 Number 111½, High Street; 13 Old Courthouse; 14 Old Hastings House; 15 Piece of Cheese House; 16 Pulpitt Gate; 17 St Clement's Caves; 18 St Clement's church; 19 St Mary in the Castle; 20 St Mary Star of the Sea; 21 Sea Life Centre; 22 Shipwreck Heritage Centre; 23 Shovells; 24 Smugglers Adventure; 25 Stables Theatre; 26 Stag inn; 27 Torfield; 28 Wellington House; 29 Ye Olde Pumpe House.

interesting wooden net shops which date from Tudor times and are unique to Hastings. The harbour exists in name only as the boats have to be drawn up on the beach, but there is an active fishing fleet and fresh fish can be bought on the beach.

Westwards, the seafront possesses the usual seaside amenities and leads to the newer part of Hastings, which started its development in the early nineteenth century, but much of it is now the modern shopping area. Beyond this, the front has an attractive promenade behind the shingle beach and a good pier which dates from 1872.

Continuing westwards, Hastings merges into **St Leonards** at Warrior Square, a formal garden laid out in 1853. St Leonards was created by James Burton and his more famous son, Decimus, as a successful piece of speculative development. Intended to be an exclusive residential area, there are some attractive buildings along the front and inland, but the development is marred by the modernistic development of Marine Court, which was built in 1937–8.

Old Town walk

Start at Rock-a-Nore at the far eastern end of the town. This is very much a working beach and you can watch the fishing boats leaving or returning. Behind the beach, the high sandstone cliffs stretch away eastwards for over 4 miles (6.5 km) to Pett Level. Fulmars and other seabirds nest in the cliffs.

From Rock-a-Nore, pass the Sea Life Centre and the Shipwreck Heritage Centre and on the right is the East Cliff Railway, which climbs to the top of the cliffs and the start of

All Saints Street in Hastings Old Town.

The net shops and Fisherman's Museum, Hastings.

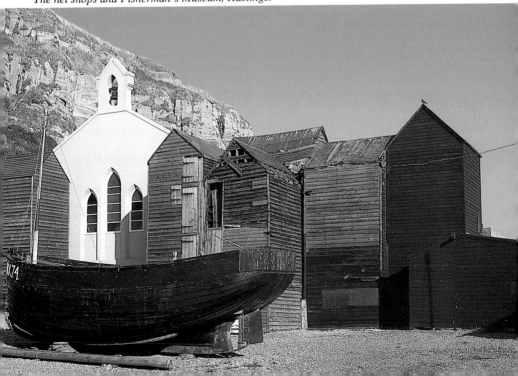

the Hastings Country Park, which stretches to Fairlight. Or you can climb Tamarisk Steps instead. Further along are the Fisherman's Museum, housed in a church dating from 1854, and the net shops. Opposite these is the Mermaid, once the headquarters of the Winkle Club; formed in 1832, this charitable organisation requires its members to carry a winkle shell in their pockets at all times and if challenged by a fellow member with the cry 'Up winkle' they must produce it or pay a fine.

Next turn into All Saints' Street, with its high pavements and many timber-framed buildings. The medieval-looking building at the start, Pulpitt Gate, is not original but was built in 1953 using old materials. A number of narrow streets and alleys run eastwards up the cliff and are worth exploring as they show how crammed in were the houses on this side of the valley.

Along Starrs Cottages lies the Piece of Cheese House, its shape determined by the available land. There are a number of good timber-framed houses including Shovells, once the home of the mother of Admiral Sir Cloudsley Shovell and dating from about 1500. Further along, the Stag inn was built about 1600 and opposite is All Saints' Cottage with timbering in its natural colour. Off to the right, Ebenezer Road leads steeply up to the Ebenezer Chapel, which dates from 1817.

All Saints' church dates from about 1400 but was much restored in 1870. It retains some interesting features inside including fine ribbed vaulting in the tower, and the remains of a Doom painting above the chancel arch. The notorious Titus Oates, who in 1678 concocted the Popish Plot which led to a wave of persecutions, was baptised in All Saints' in 1619 and was later curate there.

Cross Bourne Road, once the bed of the Bourne Stream, which is now diverted underground in pipes, to the High Street, running parallel to All Saints' Street. At the beginning of High Street are two very fine houses, Torfield and Old Hastings House, both dating from around 1750. Opposite lies the Stables Theatre, housed in the original stables to Old Hastings House, and next to these is the Catholic church of St Mary Star of the Sea,

which dates from 1882. The old part of the High Street starts here with another high pavement and a good collection of buildings, many timber-framed and others with Georgian bow-fronted windows. Immediately on the left is the house where Dante Gabriel Rossetti lived in 1854, and next to it the fine Georgian-fronted Apothecary House. High Street was the commercial heart of the old town and still has many shops, including antique and bric-a-brac shops for endless browsing. Quaint little alleyways lead up the hill to other houses on higher levels; in particular, look through the wrought-iron gateway of Number 111½.

Further down on the left, Courthouse Lane leads back to Bourne Road, near the corner of which is the Old Courthouse, dating from 1450 and said to be the oldest secular building in Hastings.

Back in the High Street stands the Old Town Hall Museum and by its side is Church Passage, which leads to St Clement's church, dating from 1380. Turn along Church Passage, with its attractive little cottages, and into Croft Road; Cobourg Place leads to the top of West Hill and to the castle and St Clement's Caves. Continue past the church back to the High Street and opposite is Wellington House, which was the headquarters of Arthur Wellesley, later Duke of Wellington, in 1806.

Turn right into George Street, which is now pedestrianised. In a short distance is Ye Olde Pumpe House, which is not medieval but built in the 1950s and very overdone. By the side, some steps lead steeply up to the top of West Hill. If you are feeling fit, this is the best route because it takes you up via Hill Street and Exmouth Place, both built when Hastings was at the height of its popularity as a resort, and in which are some very elegant houses. At the end of Exmouth Place is the former house of Dr Elizabeth Blackwell, the first woman in the world to qualify as a doctor; she retired to Hastings and died in 1910. If you want an easier way up, continue along George Street and take the West Hill lift.

At the top, continue past the castle and down Castle Hill to Wellington Square, dating from the 1820s, and the modern shopping area, then back along the seafront to Rock-a-

Nore. On the left, note the very fine Regency Pelham Crescent and in the centre the church of St Mary in the Castle, dating from 1824 and built right into the cliff. It is now being restored. Also, look above the shop fronts and you can still see in places the old buildings of the fishing town.

Castle, page 70; **cliff railways**, page 106; **Fisherman's Museum**, page 100; **Hastings Embroidery**, page 112; **Hastings Museum and Art Gallery**, page 100; **Museum of Local History**, page 100; **Sea Life Centre**, page 112; **Shipwreck Heritage Centre**, page 100; **Smugglers Adventure**, page 112.

In the locality: Battle Abbey, page 73; Bodiam Castle, page 68; Brickwall House, page 83; Carr Taylor Vineyard, page 113; Footland Wood, page 60; Fore Wood, page 61; Great Dixter, page 85; Kent & East Sussex Railway, page 107; Leeford Vineyards, page 114; Quarry Farm Rural Experience, page 112; Sedlescombe Vineyard, page 114.

Haywards Heath

Early closing Wednesday; market day Friday.

This flourishing market town owes its existence to the refusal of Cuckfield and Lindfield to have a railway through them. The railway was built across a stretch of heathland between them and the town grew up around it. It is a pleasant residential area with some good parks, and the railway still plays an important role for the residents, many of whom commute to London. Having been established only since 1841, the town has little of architectural importance, but there is a good modern shopping area.

During the Civil War, at the battle of Haywards Heath, a Royalist force was routed with the loss of more than two hundred lives.

Lindfield, now entirely surrounded by Haywards Heath, retains its village atmosphere and has long been regarded as one of the most picturesque of Sussex villages. A long main street full of attractive houses and inns, many of them timber-framed, runs from the thirteenth-century church at one end to the most attractive village pond and common at the other. The village did

not always present such an idyllic scene. After the Napoleonic Wars many of the inhabitants were in a state of great poverty. In 1824 William Allen, a Quaker, settled in the village and set up a number of smallholdings, which he let, with cottage and stock, for four shillings per week to help to relieve poverty.

In the locality: Bluebell Railway, page 106; Borde Hill Garden, page 83; Chailey Windmill, page 106; Priest House, West Hoathly, page 90; Rock Lodge Vineyard, page 114; Sheffield Park, page 91; Wakehurst Place, page 94.

Heathfield

Early closing Wednesday; market day Tuesday.

This pleasant town grew up around the railway, which has now deserted it, but it continues to flourish and is now a rapidly expanding residential area.

To the east of the town is the expanse of Heathfield Park, once the home of General Elliott, who was created Lord Heathfield for his defence of Gibraltar in 1779–82. Beyond the park is Old Heathfield, the original village, with some attractive cottages and the excellent Star Inn clustered around the thirteenth-century church. One item of particular interest in the church is the modern stained glass window showing American Indians watching Robert Hunt, vicar of Heathfield and chaplain to the Virginia expedition of 1606, administer Holy Communion.

Half a mile (800 metres) east of Old

The Jack Cade memorial at Cade Street, near Heathfield.

Heathfield lies the hamlet of **Cade Street**, which is said to be the site where Jack Cade was killed by the Sheriff of Kent after his rebellion in 1450. There is a stone marker on the site and the nearby pub is called the Jack Cade. However, despite the temptation to associate the names, Cade Street seems to have been in existence at least a century before Jack's time.

In the locality: Bateman's, page 83; Cuckoo Trail, page 59; Hidden Spring Vineyard, page 114; Merrydown Wine Company, page 114; St George's Vineyard, page 114.

Herstmonceux

Herstmonceux Castle, page 70; church of All Saints, page 79; Thomas Smith's Trug Shop, page 113.

Horsham

Early closing Thursday.

This flourishing and expanding market town prospered in the thirteenth century as an ironworking centre of the western Weald. It has recently seen much expansion and is an important residential and shopping area.

The central redevelopment has attempted to integrate many of the old streets with the new shopping precincts and car parks and there are a number of attractive streets and alleys.

Behind the old town hall lies the best of the streets, The Causeway, a delightful cul-de-sac which leads to the church. It was so named because it was originally built on wooden piles above marshes. It is solid now, though, and lined with delightful timber-framed and tile-hung houses, a number of them roofed appropriately with Horsham slate. In one of these is housed Horsham Museum. The church dates in part from the twelfth century.

A mile (1.6 km) from the town is Christ's Hospital, the famous Bluecoat School, which was founded in London in 1552 by Edward VI. The school moved to Horsham in 1902 and the present building incorporates parts of the London building.

Horsham Museum, page 100.

In the locality: Bookers Vineyard, page 113; Blue Idol Meeting House, page 76; High Beeches, page 86; King's Mill, page 108; Leonardslee, page 87; Mannings Heath

hammer ponds, page 108; Nymans Garden, page 88; Shipley hammer pond, page 109.

Hove

See under Brighton, page 22.

Hurstpierpoint

Washbrooks Farm Centre, page 113.

Ifield

See under Crawley, page 29.

Lancing

See under Worthing, page 56.

Lewes

Early closing Wednesday; market day Monday.

The county town of East Sussex and once the county town for the whole county before division, Lewes is a pleasant market town on the banks of the Ouse. Attractively situated on a spur of the Downs overlooking the Ouse valley, its naturally defensive position made it an important place from Saxon times. With the arrival of the Normans, the town was given to William de Warrene, who built the massive castle which dominates the town and a priory which was destroyed at the Dissolution of the Monasteries in 1536.

Many of the buildings in Lewes are timber-framed with Georgian façades and it is in Lewes that 'mathematical tiles' can be seen at their best. These were designed to imitate the more fashionable brick. Also, look out for imposing 'stone' doorways and quoin 'stones' that are actually painted wood. With its closeness to the Downs, flint is much in evidence in Lewes and another Lewes architectural speciality is the use of grey header bricks which are formed by the action of wood ash during firing.

Town walk

Start at Westgate car park. Notice high up on the wall a white lion, the sign from an inn of that name which once occupied the site. Go into the High Street and immediately on the right is a double bow-fronted house, which is actually a later façade on a timber-framed building. Nextdoor is the former home of

Lewes Castle.

Thomas Paine (1737–1809), author of *The Rights of Man* and, later, one of the authors of the American Declaration of Independence. Further along the High Street, on the left, is Pipe Passage, named after the clay-pipe kiln which stood near here in the nineteenth century. There are many of these narrow alleyways, called twittens locally, which lead off the High Street and are well worth exploring.

Further on, St Michael's church is built of squared knapped flint and has a thirteenth-century round tower, one of only three in Sussex. They are all in the Ouse valley, the others being at Southease and Piddinghoe. Just past the church is the home of Dr Gideon Mantell, who was born in Lewes in 1790 and discovered the first *Iguanodon* skeleton in Tilgate Forest.

Then walk to the castle entrance; to the left of the barbican gateway is Barbican House, a beautiful example of the use of black mathematical tiles. On the opposite side of the road, Number 72 has a fine Georgian front, but look down the twitten at the side and the overhanging jetty reveals its earlier origins.

Nextdoor, Number 74 has some medieval window frames in the side elevation. Further along is the White Hart Inn, a fine old coaching inn and a favourite debating venue for Thomas Paine, and opposite is the original County Hall, now court rooms. Off to the left, Fisher Street leads past the former Star brewery and to the Old Needlemakers craft centre, which is housed in the former works.

Back in the High Street, at the junction with Market Street continue straight ahead and steeply downhill. On the corner of Market Street, the Crown Hotel has a very fine Venetian window above the entrance. Just past Market Street on the left is a plaque commemorating the Protestant martyrs who were burnt at the stake near here during the Marian persecutions of 1555–7. Lewes has a famous bonfire parade and fireworks display on 5th November to commemorate them.

At the bottom of the High Street cross over into Cliffe High Street, which has now been pedestrianised. Cliffe was once a separate village. On the left is the very fine eighteenth-century Dial House and further on is the bridge over the river Ouse. Lewes was once a thriv-

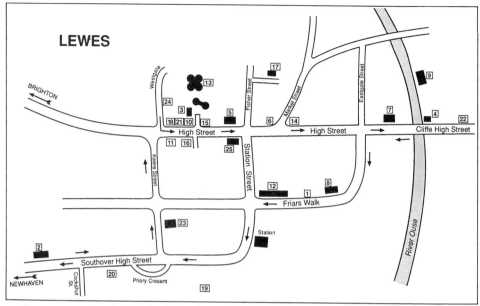

Lewes street plan: 1 All Saints' church; 2 Anne of Cleves House; 3 Barbican House; 4 Bridge House; 5 Courts (former County Hall); 6 Crown Hotel; 7 Dial House; 8 Friends' Meeting House; 9 Harvey's brewery; 10 House of Dr Gideon Mantell; 11 House of Thomas Paine; 12 Lansdowne Place; 13 Lewes Castle; 14 Memorial to Protestant martyrs; 15 Museum of Sussex Archaeology; 16 Numbers 72-4, High Street; 17 Old Needlemakers craft centre; 18 Pipe Passage; 19 Priory of St Pancras; 20 St John the Baptist's church; 21 St Michael's church; 22 St Thomas à Becket's church; 23 Southover Grange; 24 Westgate car park; 25 White Hart inn.

ing port but many of the old warehouses are now being converted to shops and craft centres. From the bridge there is a good view of Harvey's brewery, founded in 1790, and, on the other side, of Bridge House with its attractive slate coverings.

Continue along Cliffe High Street, which contains some attractive buildings, to the church of St Thomas à Becket, which dates in part from the thirteenth century, and then retrace your steps back over the bridge to Friars Walk and turn left. Friars Walk is mostly residential but on the right is the Friends' Meeting House, dating from 1784, which again demonstrates some fine use of mathematical tiles. Just past this is All Saints' church, now an arts and youth centre, and further on is Lansdowne Place, a very fine terrace dating from 1827. On the corner of the terrace is the Lansdowne Arms; note the round end to the brickwork, a feature much seen in

Lewes but not generally common in England.

Turn left, past the station, into Southover High Street and pass Priory Crescent, built around 1840. Next to that is the church of St John the Baptist, formerly part of the priory of St Pancras, and in a short distance Cockshut Street leads off to the left to the remains of the priory. A short distance further along the High Street lies the very fine Anne of Cleves House, now a museum.

Opposite Priory Crescent, a narrow street leads back to the castle, passing Southover Grange. This was built in 1572 with stone from the priory and was the home from 1630 to 1637 of John Evelyn, the diarist, whilst he attended the nearby grammar school. The gardens of the Grange are most attractive and well worth a visit.

Continue back to Lewes High Street up Keere Street, the oldest cobbled street in the town. The Prince Regent, later George IV, is said to have once driven a coach and horses down here for a bet, which must have been hard on the horses.

At the High Street, Westgate can be seen just to the right, but the rest of the High Street to the west is also worth exploring.

Anne of Cleves House Museum, page 101; **Lewes Castle**, page 70; **Lewes Priory**, page 74; **Museum of Sussex Archaeology**, page 102.

In the locality: Bentley Wildfowl and Motor Museum, page 110; Breaky Bottom Vineyard, page 113; Chailey Windmill, page 106; Clayton church, page 78; Clayton Windmills, page 106; Ditchling Beacon, page 60; Firle Place, page 84; Glynde church, page 79; Glynde Place, page 84; Lavender Line, page 108; Monk's House, page 87; Mount Caburn, page 67.

Lindfield

See under Haywards Heath, page 35.

Litlington

See under Wilmington, page 54.

Littlehampton

Early closing Wednesday.

Situated at the mouth of the river Arun, Littlehampton was an important port as far back as Saxon times. It was the port for Arundel in the middle ages and a royal shipyard in the time of Henry VIII. In the early nineteenth century it achieved some popularity as a seaside resort but never acquired the fashionable terraces or patronage of other resorts.

The lovely sandy beaches, safe bathing and proximity to the Downs make it a popular resort today. The harbour, whilst not the important commercial port of former times, is, like all harbours, a constant source of interest.

The town is pleasant, although there is little of great architectural interest. The seafront is half a mile (800 metres) away and between the town and the sea is the Green, a large undeveloped open space, an unusual feature in a seaside resort.

On the west bank of the river is West Beach, leading to Climping beach, an unspoilt area of beach and sand dunes which is the home of seabirds and some rare flowers.

Left: *Harvey's Brewery, Lewes, and the river Ouse.*
Right: *Keere Street, Lewes, down which the Prince Regent is said to have driven a coach and four.*

Littlehampton Museum, page 102; **West Beach**, page 63.

In the locality: Arundel Vineyards, page 113; Burpham church, page 76; Climping church, page 78; Ford church, page 79; Highdown Gardens, page 86; Highdown Hill, page 66.

Lullington

Church, page 80; Lullington Heath Nature Reserve, page 61.

Lurgashall

Lying remotely in wooded country north of Petworth, this is the quintessential English village. Picturesque cottages, mostly stone and tile-hung, are gathered around a large triangular village green. The pub, unusually called the Noah's Ark, sits next to the church in best village tradition.

The church dates from the eleventh century, but it has been much restored. Of particular note is the unusual lean-to timber gallery added in the sixteenth century.

Lurgashall Winery, page 114.

In the locality: Blackdown, page 58; Easebourne Priory, page 73; Petworth House, page 90; The Mens, page 61.

Mayfield

This hilltop village has one of the most charming High Streets in the county. Once at the heart of the Wealden iron industry, the village later became an important coaching stage but has been greatly enhanced since the bypass removed much of the through traffic. The High Street tumbles down the hillside with brick pavements lined either side with timber-framed, tile-hung and white weatherboarded buildings. The Middle House Hotel is an especially fine timber-framed inn dating from 1575.

At the north end is a Roman Catholic girls' school which incorporates the remains of a former palace of the Archbishops of Canterbury, including a magnificent medieval hall. It is said to have been founded originally by St Dunstan in the tenth century and it was in Mayfield that he is reputed to have pinched the nose of the Devil. The last Archbishop to own it was Thomas Cranmer, who made it

over to Henry VIII in 1545. St Dunstan and the Devil are depicted on the village sign.

The large airy parish church of St Dunstan dates in part from the thirteenth century but was rebuilt in 1389 and has been added to since. The chancel has been much restored, but the nave retains its rough-dressed stone fabric. There is some fine vaulting and some iron tomb slabs, relics of the iron industry. In the west wall is a memorial window to Sir John Bagot Glubb (1897–1986), the soldier, who became known as 'Glubb Pasha' during his distinguished career in the Middle East.

In the locality: Ashdown Forest, page 57; Bartley Mill, page 105; Bayham Abbey, page 73; Bewl Water, page 58; St George's Vineyard, page 114.

Midhurst

Early closing Wednesday.

This delightful town has developed in two distinct phases. The main road, North Street, is wide and spacious with some attractive Georgian frontages, but behind this lies the medieval part around South Street and the Market Place. There are some very good timber-framed houses in South Street; most prominent is the lovely Spread Eagle, a large coaching inn dating from the fifteenth century, with a seventeenth-century front. The Angel Hotel is said to have been given its name by the Pilgrim Fathers who stayed there on their way to Southampton to embark for the Americas. The church, which dates in part from the twelfth century, was much restored in 1881.

Coming right up to the town are the grounds of Cowdray Park, the seat of Viscount Cowdray. The present house dates from the nineteenth century but in the park are the remains of the Tudor mansion which was started in 1492 and completed by Sir Anthony Browne. Sir Anthony was granted Battle Abbey at the Dissolution (see page 73) and as the monks were being ejected they laid a curse upon him that his house would be destroyed by fire and water. The curse was slow to be fulfilled, but in 1793 the house burnt down and a week later the last of Sir Anthony's descendants was drowned. The remains of the house now make a romantic ruin and the

Eastbourne, from the pier.

Bury was the home of John Galsworthy.

The Spread Eagle Hotel at Midhurst is an ancient coaching inn.

England. Fortunately this never happened and the town remained small and the river unspoilt.

Architecturally, the town is not especially attractive but it is full of interest, as all busy ports are. The Bridge Hotel, which dates from the seventeenth century, was the stopping place for Louis Philippe on his escape from the French uprising in 1848. The parish church has a Norman tower and apse but was heavily restored in 1854. In the churchyard is a gravestone to Thomas Tipper, the brewer of Tipper's ale, with an amusing inscription.

Garden Paradise and Planet Earth, page 112; **Newhaven Fort,** page 72; **Newhaven Local and Maritime History Museum,** page 102.

In the locality: Bishopstone church, page 76; Breaky Bottom Vineyard, page 113; Charleston Farmhouse, page 83; Firle Place, page 84; Glynde church, page 79; Glynde Place, page 84; Monk's House, page 87; Mount Caburn, page 67; Piddinghoe church, page 80.

grounds are a very attractive place to walk and watch polo.

The Cowdray Estate owns much of the surrounding land and property in many villages; the latter is easily identified by the vivid yellow paint on the woodwork.

In the locality: Blackdown, page 58; Chilsdown Vineyard, page 113; Coultershaw Water Pump, page 106; Easebourne Priory, page 73; Petworth House, page 90; Weald and Downland Open Air Museum, page 104; West Dean Gardens, page 94.

Newhaven
Early closing Wednesday.
This busy cross-Channel port at the mouth of the river Ouse is now the only passenger port of any importance in Sussex. A haven of some sort had existed at the little village of Meeching since Roman times, but from Elizabethan times the 'New Haven' started to develop. The railway company chose Newhaven, rather than Littlehampton, as its main Sussex port and at one time it was proposed to turn the entire stretch of river between the port and Lewes into the Liverpool of southern

Ninfield
Cast-iron stocks, page 108.

Northiam
This large strung-out village has suffered much development at the northern end, but the old centre clustered around the village green is still delightful with much white weatherboarding in evidence. On the green stands an old thatched well-house and nearby is an oak tree, much braced and supported, under which Queen Elizabeth I is said to have picnicked in 1573 on the way to Rye. At the edge of the green is an unusual three-storeyed timber-framed building.

The church of St Mary has been much restored, but it does retain one of the few stone spires left in the county.

Bodiam Ferry Company, page 110; **Brickwall House,** page 83; **Great Dixter,** page 85; **Kent & East Sussex Railway,** page 107.

In the locality: Bodiam Castle, page 68; Farm World, page 111; Footland Wood, page 60; Quarry Farm Rural Experience, page 112; Sedlescombe Vineyard, page 114.

North Marden

Church of St Mary, page 80.

Penhurst

Church of St Michael, page 80.

Petworth

Early closing Wednesday.

On the slopes of the Greensand Ridge north of the Downs, this picturesque little town sits closely huddled against the walls of Petworth House. Not much bigger than a village, the heart of Petworth is a delightful jumble of narrow streets and alleys centred on the little market square. Many of the streets follow the medieval town plan, and Lombard Street, which is typical, carried the main drain in an open gully down the centre.

There are numerous attractive buildings, including many that are timber-framed and tile-hung. The parish church was originally built in the fourteenth century but was rebuilt in 1827. In 1947 a rather spindly spire was removed because it was unsafe, but replaced by an incongruous top.

Traffic is the big problem in Petworth. Lying at the junction of several main roads, the narrow twisting streets create obstacles to through traffic. A bypass has been mooted for years, but since the authorities' choice is through Petworth Park it is unsurprisingly meeting with opposition.

Petworth House, page 90.

In the locality: Bignor Roman Villa, page 65; Blackdown, page 58; Burton Mill, page 106; Coultershaw Water Pump, page 106; Easebourne Priory, page 73; Hardham church, page 79; Lurgashall Winery, page 114; The Mens, page 61.

Pevensey

Early closing Thursday.

This ancient village was originally built on a small *ey* or island, which was surrounded by sea on three sides. The sea now lies over a mile away and the village is surrounded by the marshland of Pevensey Levels.

This is one of the most historic places in Sussex, for as *Anderida* it was the strong point in the Roman defences and, a thousand years later, was to become the landing place of William the Conqueror in 1066. Following the Norman Conquest, Pevensey became part of the Cinque Ports and as a 'Limb' of Hastings continued to send one ship for the king's service for some time despite the problems of silting. Pevensey retained its mayor and corporation, despite its diminutive size, until 1883 and the Court House in the main street was once the town hall and is claimed to be the smallest in England. The Old Mint House, now an antique shop, dates from the fourteenth century, but a mint was on the site as early as 1076. A bypass has now removed much of the traffic from the historic centre.

Pevensey Castle, page 43.

In the locality: Abbot's Wood, page 57; Filching Manor Motor Museum, page 99; Herstmonceux Castle, page 70; Herstmonceux church, page 79; Thomas Smith's Trug Shop, page 113; Michelham Priory, page 74; Polegate Windmill, page 109.

Piddinghoe

Church of St John, page 80.

Piltdown

See under Fletching, page 31.

Polegate

Polegate Windmill, page 109; Filching Manor Motor Museum, page 99.

Poynings

Pronounced locally as 'Punnings', this small downland village is tucked under the north face of the Downs below Devil's Dyke. It takes its name from the Poyngges family, early lords of the manor. The third Lord Poyngges, Michael (died 1368), fought at Crécy and Poitiers and left money in his will to rebuild the church.

Set on the lower slopes of the Downs, the church is large, cruciform and built mainly in Perpendicular style. The inside is plain and relatively unrestored and the transeptal crossing arches are very fine.

Further west lie the small villages of **Fulking** and **Edburton** which, like Poynings, are on the spring line of the Downs. Water percolating through the porous chalk of the

A downland spring at Fulking.

Downs meets the impermeable clay at their base and gushes out. This is especially apparent by the side of the Shepherd and Dog public house at Fulking. It was this effect which was to a large extent responsible for the flooding at Chichester early in 1994.

In the locality: Devil's Dyke, page 65; Newtimber Place, page 88.

Pulborough
Early closing Wednesday; market day Monday.

This small market town, situated at the point where the Roman road Stane Street crosses the river Arun, was an important site during the Roman occupation, judging by the remains found in the area. Although at the crossroads of the London to Chichester and the Brighton to Winchester roads, it has not developed into a town of any size. There are two distinct parts to the town, the lower one, with some pretty houses and inns, by the river and the upper part around the church. The church dates from the fourteenth century and has a good king-post roof and a lychgate which is contemporary with the church.

A mile or so to the west is the medieval bridge at **Stopham**, which has now had the traffic removed from it.

In the locality: Amberley Chalk Pits Museum, page 95; Bignor Roman Villa, page 65; Coultershaw Water Pump, page 106; Hardham church, page 79; Hollygate Cactus Nursery, page 112; Nutbourne Vineyard, page 114; Parham House, page 89; Petworth House, page 90; Pulborough Brooks RSPB Reserve, page 62; The Mens, page 61.

Ringmer

This large village has seen much development over recent years but has managed to retain its large village green complete with cricket field. The area around the church and green is quite pleasing and flint is much in evidence with its closeness to the Downs. The church dates in part from the thirteenth century and, although restored in 1884, retains many interesting features, including two attractive side chapels built in

Opposite: *The church of St Peter ad Vincula at Wisborough Green.*

Perpendicular style.

Gilbert White, the naturalist, visited his aunt, Rebecca Snooke, in Ringmer. He dated many of his letters from here and immortalised her tortoise, Timothy. Timothy's home, Delves House, a fine Georgian building, is still in existence and lies a short distance from the church, on the green. The village was also the home of Gulielma Springett, who married William Penn in 1672, and of Ann Sadler, who married John Harvard in 1636. Both families were later to become involved in the early development of the United States of America. The village sign incorporates references to them and to Timothy.

A mile (1.6 km) south of the village is the internationally famous opera house at Glyndebourne.

In the locality: Bentley Wildfowl and Motor Museum, page 110; Firle Place, page 84; Glynde church, page 79; Glynde Place, page 84; Lavender Line, page 108; Mount Caburn, page 67.

Cricket bats have been made in Robertsbridge for over a century.

Robertsbridge

Situated north of Battle, Robertsbridge has at last been bypassed, allowing its fine collection of medieval houses to be viewed in comparative safety. From the George Inn at the south end, where Belloc sat 'gazing into the fire and drinking their fine port', and the crossing of the river Rother further north is an attractive collection of timber-framed and tile-hung buildings.

The village has been famous for its cricket bats for more than a century. Many famous cricketers have used Robertsbridge bats, from W. G. Grace to the West Indian Brian Lara, who made his record-breaking 375 test runs in April 1994 using a Robertsbridge bat.

There is no parish church in Robertsbridge; this lies at **Salehurst**, a mile (1.6 km) away, which was the original village from before Domesday until a 'new' bridge in the twelfth century shifted the focus around the river crossing. There is little at Salehurst now except the church, a pub and a handful of pleasant cottages.

The church dates in part from the fourteenth century and in the churchyard are some eighteenth-century table tombs with terracotta plaques by Jonathan Harmer. Inside, the main items of interest are some iron tomb slabs, the font, said to have been given by Richard the Lionheart, and some fine medieval glass with representations of birds.

Robertsbridge Abbey, page 75; **Museum of Rural Life**, page 102.

In the locality: Bateman's, page 83; Bodiam Castle, page 68; Etchingham church, page 78; Footland Wood, page 60; Haremere Hall, page 86; Quarry Farm Rural Experience, page 112.

Rottingdean

Lying on the eastern outskirts of Brighton, Rottingdean has retained a village-like atmosphere in its centre. Sir Edward Burne-Jones and Rudyard Kipling took up residence here; the former is buried in the church, but Kipling became tired of day trippers from Brighton peeping over his garden wall and decamped to Burwash.

There are some pretty houses grouped around the village pond and church, which in

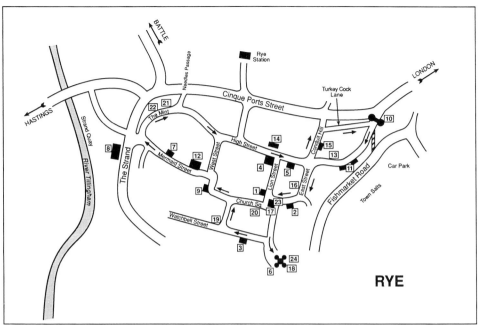

Rye street plan: 1 Fletcher's House; 2 Flushing Inn; 3 Friars of the Sack; 4 George Hotel; 5 Gill's House; 6 Gun Garden; 7 Harts Horn House; 8 Heritage Centre; 9 Lamb House; 10 Landgate; 11 Lookouts; 12 Mermaid Inn; 13 Number 1, High Street (ironmonger); 14 Old Grammar School; 15 Old Monastery; 16 Old Vicarage Hotel; 17 Old Water House; 18 Rye Museum; 19 St Anthony's, 20 St Mary's church; 21 Standard Inn; 22 Swan Cottage; 23 Town Hall; 24 Ypres Tower (castle).

parts dates from Norman times but was completely restored by Sir George Gilbert Scott in 1856. Burne-Jones designed the stained glass, which was manufactured in the workshops of William Morris.

Rottingdean is the home of the Copper family, who have endeavoured to keep alive the traditional Sussex folk-songs. Bob Copper's autobiographical *Early to Rise* evokes the flavour of life in a small Sussex village between the two world wars.

Rottingdean Grange, page 102.

In the locality: Breaky Bottom Vineyard, page 113; Monk's House, page 87; South Downs Way, page 62.

Rye

Early closing Tuesday; market day Thursday; cattle market Wednesday.

Built on a hilltop at the end of one of the

Southern Forest Ridges, Rye is the most eastern port in Sussex. It was not one of the original Cinque Ports, but in 1346, along with Winchelsea, it was appointed as an 'Antient Town'. However, as the sea receded, the town diminished in importance as a port. Rye was sacked by the French in the fourteenth and fifteenth centuries and was largely rebuilt in the sixteenth. It is mainly this period, with Georgian additions, which is delightfully represented in Rye today. The narrow streets, many of them cobbled, are crammed with attractive buildings, many of them timber-framed, making Rye one of the most picturesque towns in Sussex.

Rye is the perfect example of an ancient town but it is not a museum; it is a living, bustling town and still, despite the problems of silting in the river, administers a busy port.

Town walk

Start at the Landgate, with its 40 feet (12 metres) high twin drum towers, and the only survivor of four gates built in 1340 when the town was fortified against the French.

Walking into the town, two lookouts give excellent views over the river and surrounding countryside. Below, the area now occupied by the car park and recreation grounds was originally the town salts, which were allowed to flood with sea water and evaporate to provide salt, a valuable commodity in the past. It was last under water in 1823.

Number 1 High Street is said to be one of the oldest ironmongers in England, dating from 1640. The buildings here are a pleasant collection of architectural styles, including some Georgian façades over earlier buildings. Look above shop fronts and you can sometimes see that the building is much older than the façade suggests; money was often not spent above eye level when fashions changed.

East Street has a number of timber-framed buildings and a fine Georgian brick building, the Old Vicarage Hotel. Turn into Market Street, past the Flushing Inn, dating from the fifteenth century, and at the bottom is the Town Hall, dating from 1742.

To the left in Lion Street, named after the Red Lion inn which stood on the site of the nineteenth-century school, is the parish church of St Mary. On the right is Fletcher's House, which is built on the site of the old vicarage in which John Fletcher, the dramatist, was born in 1579.

The church is partly Norman and a feature of particular interest is the clock, made in Winchelsea in 1560, and claimed to be the oldest church turret-clock in England. The face is flanked by two quarter-boys which strike the bells on the quarter hours. If the tower is open, take the opportunity to go up, for there are spectacular views.

To the left, the very fine oval brick structure is the Old Water House, the town reservoir, dating from 1736. In the left-hand corner of Church Square is the Ypres Tower, a castle built in 1258 to defend the harbour

Opposite: From Rye church tower, a gilt quarter-boy and Rye rooftops.

below. It is named after Thomas Ypres, who bought it in 1430, and now houses a small museum. To the side of the tower is the Gun Garden, a gun battery to defend the harbour, again giving splendid views.

On the left in Church Square is the Friars of the Sack, the remains of the thirteenth-century home of these friars, so called from their clothing of sackcloth. At the end of Church Square, Watchbell Street leads downhill, but turn right to finish off Church Square; on the corner is St Anthony's, a very fine timber-framed building. Go left into West Street, at the end of which is the attractive Georgian brick building called Lamb House, formerly the home of Henry James and later of another writer, E. H. Benson.

From West Street, Mermaid Street, probably the most photographed street in the county, tumbles down to the quayside. It is filled with attractive houses, amongst them the Mermaid Inn, which dates from the fifteenth century, and Harts Horn House, a fifteenth-century three-storey gabled house which was used as a hospital in the Napoleonic Wars. Near the bottom, on the left, Trader's Passage runs around the cliff face above the harbour. At the bottom, the old warehouses on Strand Quay have now been converted into an attractive area of shops and restaurants and one houses the Heritage Centre.

To the right lies The Mint, so named because coins were minted here in the seventeenth century. It leads back to the High Street. Swan Cottage, dating from 1420, has some examples of pargeting and by the side of the Standard Inn a narrow passageway gives a glimpse of what a medieval town was like.

The George Hotel hides a sixteenth-century building behind its attractive Georgian exterior and opposite is the former Old Grammar School, given by Sir Thomas Peacocke in 1636 as a free school for the town. Just past Lion Street on the right is the house of Gill, clockmakers 1630–1791, and Daniel Gill, banker, 1791.

Go left down Conduit Hill, past the Old Monastery, now a pottery, but part of a larger building originally built as a chapel of the Friars Heremites of St Augustine in 1379. Turn

New Shoreham from across the river Adur.

right along Turkey Cock Lane, along the line of the old town walls, and back to the Landgate.

Rye Heritage Centre, page 103; **Lamb House**, page 86; **Martello Towers**, page 71; **Rye Museum**, page 103.

In the locality: Brickwall House, page 82; Camber Castle, page 69; Farm World, page 111; Great Dixter, page 85; Kent & East Sussex Railway, page 107; Royal Military Canal, page 72; Rye Harbour Nature Reserve, page 62.

St Leonards

See under Hastings, page 31.

Salehurst

See under Robertsbridge, page 46.

Seaford

Early closing Wednesday.

This comparatively modern resort has a quiet atmosphere; there are 3 miles (5 km) of seafront with good views, bathing and other facilities, but there is neither a pier nor any large amusement arcade. It was once the main port on the river Ouse and, as a 'Limb' of Hastings, an important part of the Cinque Ports confederation, until the river was diverted to Newhaven in the sixteenth century.

There are few ancient buildings in the town now, although the parish church dates in part from Norman times, but on the outskirts is the lovely Saxon church at Bishopstone.

Amongst the attractions of Seaford is the magnificent stretch of cliff downland to the east of the town, which continues to Seaford Head and the Seven Sisters Country Park in the Cuckmere valley.

Martello Tower 74, page 72.

In the locality: Bishopstone church, page 76; Charleston Farmhouse, page 83; Drusillas Park, page 111; English Wine Centre, page 114; Firle Place, page 84; Friston Forest, page 61; Long Man of Wilmington, page 66; Lullington church, page 80; Old Clergy House, page 88; Seven Sisters Country Park, page 62; South Downs Way, page 62; Wilmington Priory, page 75.

Sedlescombe

Sedlescombe Vineyard, page 114.

Shipley

Hammer pond, page109; King's Mill, page 108.

Shoreham-by-Sea

Early closing Wednesday; market day Saturday.

Shoreham has been an important port since Roman times and after the Norman Conquest became the port on the river Adur for Bramber. Old Shoreham, a mile (1.6 km) inland from the sea, has some attractive buildings clustered around the church. Nearby, the timber bridge over the river was once a toll bridge, built in 1781 and rebuilt in 1971. With the usual silting in the river, the centre of the town was moved nearer to the sea, and so New Shoreham grew up around a new church and Shoreham is unusual in having two Norman churches.

Shoreham was the landing place of King John when he returned to claim the throne after the death of Richard I and it is reputed to have been the departure point of Charles II when he left for exile in France. A once thriving oyster industry declined during the Crimean War through shortage of labour and was finally destroyed by pollution.

Around the harbour are some attractive buildings including the Marlipins, which dates from the twelfth century and is now used as a

Steyning High Street.

museum. A busy port, the nearest on the south coast to London, and the largest commercial port between Dover and Southampton, the harbour is a constant source of interest.

Marlipins Museum, page 103; **Church of St Mary de Hardura**, page 80; **Church of St Nicholas**, page 80.

In the locality: Coombes Farm Tours, page 111; Devil's Dyke, page 65; Foredown Tower, page 60; Sompting church, page 82; South Downs Way, page 62; West Blatchington Windmill, page 109; Wood's Mill Nature Reserve, page 63.

Sompting

Church of St Mary, page 82.

South Harting

South, East and West Harting are a group of three villages lying on the north side of the South Downs about 9 miles (15 km) from Chichester. There are some picturesque thatched cottages in the villages, and South Harting, which is often considered to be the most westerly village in Sussex, has an interesting early fourteenth-century church. It was much restored by Sir Gilbert Scott and the 130 feet (43 metres) high copper-sheathed spire was reconstructed after a gale in 1936. There is a war memorial in the churchyard designed by Eric Gill.

Anthony Trollope (1815–82) lived in the village for the last few years of his life.

In the locality: North Marden church, page 80; Stansted House, page 92; Uppark, page 92.

Steyning

Early closing Thursday; market day Wednesday.

This pretty market town has been much improved since the bypass removed the through traffic some years ago. There are some very attractive houses and inns, many of them timber-framed, in the High Street and the delightfully named Mouse Lane. Leading off the High Street is Church Lane, which also has many fine buildings, including the old Grammar School, which dates from 1614.

The church was founded by St Cuthman in the eighth century but was rebuilt in the eleventh century and restored in the nineteenth. St Cuthman spread the gospel through Sussex, pulling his invalid mother in a cart. In Steyning the cart broke down and Cuthman took this as a sign of where to build his church. When the cart collapsed some haymakers in a field opposite laughed and Cuthman laid a curse on the field so that it rained every time it was mown; Christianity was evidently more robust in those days! The field now houses the new buildings of the school.

Steyning Museum, page 104.

In the locality: Ashurst church, page 76; Bramber Castle, page 69; Chanctonbury Ring, page 65; Cissbury Ring, page 65; Coombes Farm Tours, page 111; Nash Vineyards, page 114; St Mary's, page 91.

Stopham
See under Pulborough, page 44.

Thakeham

Lying in quiet rural countryside, the village has some attractive buildings along the one main street and there are good views to the Downs.

The church is large for the size of the village and dates in part from Norman times but with later additions. There are some interest-ing brasses to the Aspley family and also an unusual incised tomb slab with a life-sized image of William Aspley (died 1527). Close by are some attractive timber-framed houses and thatched and Horsham-slated roofs are in evidence.

Just south of the village lies Little Thakeham, said by Nairn to be one of Sir Edwin Lutyens's best designs. It is now an hotel, but the gardens are occasionally open for charity.

Half a mile (800 metres) away by footpath across the fields lies the little church at **Warminghurst**, which was splendidly restored in 1959. The simple interior has some attractive seventeenth-century timber fittings. There are some sixteenth-century monuments to the Shelley family, ancestors of Percy Bysshe Shelley.

Warminghurst was later the home of William Penn, one the founders of Pennsylvania, but, as a Quaker, he travelled north to the Blue Idol Meeting House at Coneyhurst.

In the locality: Blue Idol Meeting House, page 76; Hollygate Cactus Nursery, page 112; King's Mill, page 108; Nutbourne Vineyard, page 114.

Three Bridges
See under Crawley, page 29.

The Doom window in Ticehurst church.

The bridge over the Rother at Trotton dates from 1400.

Ticehurst

This attractive little Wealden village on the Kent border has many white weatherboarded and tile-hung buildings. There is a small village square in front of the Duke of York and to the right of this the road leads to the church, which dates from the fourteenth century. Originally built by William de Etchingham, the church is in Perpendicular style, in contrast to that at Etchingham. It has been much restored inside but in the chancel north window are some fragments of medieval glass, apparently from a Doom window.

Ticehurst was the home for some time of Thomas Blinks (1860–1912), the artist, who specialised in sporting life pictures.

In the locality: Bayham Abbey, page 73; Bewl Water, page 58; Etchingham church, page 78; Flimwell Bird Park, page 111; Haremere Hall, page 86.

Trotton

Trotton lies 3 miles (5 km) west of Midhurst. There is little in Trotton except a few houses, a bridge and a church but the last two are of great interest. The bridge dates from about 1400 and is still carrying traffic over the river Rother. The church dates mainly from the twelfth century, but it is the interior which is of special note. Covering the whole of the west wall, and remarkably well preserved, is a series of murals depicting Christ in Judgement and the Seven Deadly Sins. There are also two very fine monumental brasses. One is to Margaret Camoys, who died about 1310, which is said to be the oldest brass to a woman in Britain. The other, larger brass is to Thomas Camoys, who fought at Agincourt, and his second wife Elizabeth, who was the widow of Sir Harry 'Hotspur' Percy (see also Petworth House, page 90).

In the locality: North Marden church, page 80; Uppark, page 92.

Twineham

Church of St Peter, page 82.

Uckfield

Early closing Wednesday.

This small market town north of Lewes was the centre of the local iron industry in the past and is now an expanding residential area. The long sloping High Street is more attractive since the bypass removed much of the through traffic. There are some pleasant buildings in the upper part, a number of which are timber-framed behind later façades; a good example is the Georgian bow-fronted Maiden's Head.

Also of note is Bridge Cottage, an aisled Wealden hall-house dating from about 1380. Acquired by the Uckfield and District Preservation Society in 1984, it has been extensively restored. The church dates in part from the fifteenth century and contains some monuments to local ironmasters, including an iron grave slab.

In the locality: Ashdown Forest, page 57; Barkham Manor Vineyard, page 113; Barnsgate Manor Vineyard, page 113; Bentley Wildfowl and Motor Museum, page 110; Bluebell Railway, page 106; Chailey Windmill, page 00; Lavender Line, page 106; Nutley Windmill, page 108; Sheffield Park, page 91.

Wadhurst

With its closeness to the main London to Hastings railway, Wadhurst has seen much development as a commuter village but has managed to retain its pleasant centre with a mixture of tile-hung and weatherboarded buildings.

The church of St Peter and St Paul has a Norman west tower and the rest is thirteenth-century but all was restored in 1858.

The village was at the heart of the Wealden iron industry and this is apparent in the interior, where there are no less than thirty iron tomb slabs set in the floor.

In the locality: Bateman's, page 83; Bartley Mill, page 105; Bayham Abbey, page 73; Bewl Water, page 58; Etchingham church, page 78; Flimwell Bird Park, page 111; Haremere Hall, page 86.

Warminghurst

See under Thakeham, page 52.

West Firle

Firle Place, page 84.

West Hoathly

Priest House, page 90.

West Tarring

See under Worthing, page 56.

West Wittering

See under the Witterings, page 56.

Wilmington

Wilmington lies either side of the A27, but the best part of the village is to the south along a narrow road which winds its way through the Downs in a gap cut by the Cuckmere river. It is one of the most attractive roads through the Downs and passes the little downland villages of Litlington and West Dean before arriving at the Seven Sisters Country Park on the coast. Also along the road is Charleston Manor, described by Pevsner as 'a perfect house in a perfect setting' and parts of which date from the early twelfth century. The manor gardens are occasionally open to the public and each summer a music festival is held in the tithe barn.

In Wilmington there are some charming flint houses in the short distance to the car park near the priory, from where there are good views of the Long Man. The village is a good walking base for the Downs.

The small flint church, with its weatherboarded bell turret, dates in part from Norman times but with many later additions. The large yew tree near the church is reputed to be over a thousand years old.

Long Man of Wilmington, page 66; Wilmington Priory, page 75.

In the locality: Abbot's Wood, page 57; Drusillas Park, page 111; English Wine Centre, page 114; Friston Forest, page 61; Hunter's Burgh, page 66; Lullington church, page 80; South Downs Way, page 62.

Winchelsea

Winchelsea was for centuries an important coastal town and, along with Rye, 2 miles (3 km) away, became a full member of the Cinque Ports in 1347. However, this is the second Winchelsea; the first, which was sited a few miles away, was severely damaged by a great storm in 1250 and finally swept away completely in 1287. Such was its importance that Edward I ordered the building of a new town, laid out on a spacious grid plan. However, although safe from the sea, its walls did not protect it from marauding French raiders and during the fourteenth and fifteenth centuries it was sacked and pillaged no less than seven times. Finally, in the sixteenth century,

The Long Man of Wilmington is 227 feet (69 metres) tall.

with the sea receding and the river silting up, Winchelsea ceased to be a port of any importance.

Although now covering only a fraction of the original site, the buildings are neat and tidy, well cared for and with an air of quiet prosperity. Some idea of the original size can be gained from the positions of the remains of three of the original gates. Of these, Strandgate is the most complete; built in the fourteenth century, it was called Strand because it originally lay by the banks of the river Brede. The steep road which passes through the gate is described by William Camden in his *Britannia* of 1586 as 'not strait lest its great declivity should make people tumble headlong as they walk down, or oblige them to go rather on all fours'.

The church of St Thomas, partially destroyed in a French raid, sits in a 2½ acre (1 hectare) site and is built in the early Decorated style. Inside, the main impression is of light and colour created by the modern (1933) windows.

Court Hall Museum, page 104.

In the locality: Camber Castle, page 69; *Royal Military Canal, page 72; Rye Harbour Nature Reserve, page 62.*

Wisborough Green

This particularly handsome village lies on the A272 around a large village green on which cricket can be watched in summer. The area round Wisborough was the centre of Sussex glassworking in the thirteenth to sixteenth centuries and traces of two furnaces have been found. The industry was mainly run by Huguenot glassworkers, refugees from persecution in France. The industry came to an end in the early seventeenth century when ordinances against burning wood were introduced.

The church of St Peter ad Vincula sits on a prominent small hill on the edge of the village and is a distinctive sight with its shingled broach spire and 'cat slide' roof. The view across the village pond is especially attractive. The church dates in part from Norman times but was restored in 1867. There is a good wall painting inside, and windows commemorate the Huguenot glassworkers and those killed in the

Dieppe raids of 1944, which were planned in the village.

In the locality: Blue Idol Meeting House, page 76; Petworth House, page 90; The Mens, page 61.

The Witterings

It is likely that the Saxons first landed in this area, on the western edge of the Selsey peninsula, but much has been engulfed by the sea. These two popular seaside resorts remain, with West Wittering being the more sedate of the two.

From West Wittering, access can be gained to Chichester Harbour and East Head, a fine expanse of beach and sand dunes now in the care of the National Trust.

In the locality: Chichester Harbour, page 59; Pagham Harbour, page 61.

Worth

Church of St Nicholas, page 82.

Worthing

Early closing Wednesday; market days Thursday and Saturday.

This flourishing seaside resort between Brighton and Littlehampton was once a small hamlet of Broadwater village. Now, however, it has one of the largest populations in Sussex and has swallowed up not only Broadwater but Durrington, West Tarring, Salvington and part of Goring. Expansion followed royal patronage, as at Brighton, but here by the younger sister of the Prince Regent, Princess Amelia. Perhaps for this reason Worthing is a much more genteel place than its boisterous neighbour.

Situated on the Coastal Plain below the southern slopes of the Downs, the town has an exceptionally mild climate and regularly enjoys more sunshine than anywhere else in Britain. The attractive esplanade has the usual amenities, including a pier, and the town also has a good theatre and maintains its own orchestra. There are some attractive Regency terraces and some older buildings survive in the former villages. **Broadwater** church is part Norman and that at **West Tarring** is Early English in style. There are also some attractive cottages in West Tarring and, nearby, the parish hall is housed in the fourteenth-century palace of the Archbishops of Canterbury.

At **Goring-by-Sea** is the house in which Richard Jefferies (1848–87) spent his last few years. Jefferies is buried in Broadwater Cemetery and his great admirer W. H. Hudson is buried nearby.

High on the Downs east of Worthing lies **Lancing** College, founded in 1848 by Canon Nathaniel Woodard, then curate of New Shoreham. Woodard founded two other schools in Sussex, at Ardingly and Hurstpierpoint, but Lancing is the most impressive architecturally. Designed by R. C. Carpenter, the Gothic Revival style buildings culminate in a chapel which is of cathedral-like proportions and which dominates the skyline on the approach from the east along the A27.

Worthing Museum and Art Gallery, page 104.

In the locality: Cissbury Ring, page 65; Coombes Farm Tours, page 111; Highdown Gardens, page 86; Highdown Hill, page 66; High Salvington Windmill, page 107; Sompting church, page 82.

57

3
Coast and countryside

Abbot's Wood (OS 199: TQ 557075). 7 miles (11 km) north of Eastbourne.

Abbot's Wood was given to Battle Abbey during the reign of Henry I and ditches and embankments from the thirteenth century are still visible in the woods. The Forestry Commission started replanting in 1953; conifers are much in evidence, but about a quarter of the forest has been planted with broad-leaved species such as oak and beech. There are rides and tracks through the woods and a waymarked trail about 2 miles (3 km) long, which passes Wilmington Lake, one of three ponds believed to have been constructed in the thirteenth century as fishponds for Battle Abbey. The wood is rich in wildlife, and of particular interest are the large nests built by wood ants. Special attention has been paid to the needs of the disabled; from the car park there is a well-surfaced level path about a quarter of a mile (400 metres) long. At regular intervals there are seats, picnic tables and information boards.

Ashdown Forest.

Ashdown Forest. 3 miles (5 km) south of East Grinstead.

Almost 14,000 acres (5600 hectares) of open heath and woodland on the high ridges of the Weald make this one of the most attractive and distinctive landscapes in southern England. In the fourteenth century the forest was so dense that sixteen guides were needed to conduct travellers from end to end. Much of the woodland has been replaced by heathland, created by felling trees for the iron industry in the sixteenth and seventeenth centuries, with the result that the light sandy soil was leached by rain and weather. There are still many trees though, and natural regeneration and woodland management are reclaiming much of the heath. Deer breed in the forest and can often be seen in the more remote areas.

Following the Restoration of the Monarchy in 1660, much of the forest was enclosed and given to the king's followers, but about 6400 acres (2500 hectares) were dedicated to the

Commoners and are freely accessible to the public; however, little grazing now takes place and this is helping the reafforestation. The forest is administered by a Board of Conservators, who maintain it as laid down in the Ashdown Forest Act, 1974, 'as a quiet and natural area of outstanding beauty'.

The forest now provides a major recreation area in the crowded south-east of England. There are numerous areas designated for picnicking, some with tables and benches, the car-parking areas generally offer magnificent views and walkers are free to go as they please. Children may perhaps recognise the settings for the adventures of Winnie-the-Pooh, for their author, A. A. Milne, lived on the edge of the forest at Hartfield. Posingford Wood and Five Hundred Acre Wood, just south of Hartfield, are the areas where most of the adventures took place and a footpath running south from Upper Hartfield to Posingford Wood crosses the bridge where Pooh and Christopher Robin played 'Poohsticks' (OS 188: TQ 470338).

Beachy Head (OS 199: TV 583952). 3 miles (5 km) south-west of Eastbourne.

At 536 feet (163 metres) this magnificent chalk headland is higher than the famous White Cliffs of Dover. The South Downs reach the sea here and end in a sheer cliff from which there are stunning views of the lighthouse sitting toy-like in the sea below. The whole of the coast between Eastbourne and Seaford is protected either by the National Trust or by local councils. The South Downs Way runs past Beachy Head and there is good walking with lovely views. Richard Jefferies often walked here for the fresh air, of which he wrote: 'It is an air without admixture. If it comes from the sea the waves refine it, if inland, the wheat and flowers distil it.' One can concur with this today.

Lying back from the headland is an interpretative centre, which has good displays covering all aspects of the area, including geology, plants, animals, sea shore, archaeology and the history of the lighthouses. There is a nature trail from the centre and the area is good for observing migrant birds and butterflies.

Bewl Water, near Lamberhurst (OS 188: TQ 686337).

With over 70 acres (28 hectares) of water, Bewl Water is the largest expanse of inland water south of the river Thames. It straddles the Kent-Sussex border and, although the entrance is on the Kent side, it provides a major leisure area for Sussex. The reservoir supplies water to mid Kent and was created by building a dam 1000 yards (900 metres) long and over 100 feet (30 metres) high across the river Bewl. Work started in 1972 and was completed in 1975. There are many fine walks, ranging from short signposted trails to the perimeter walk, which provides 15 miles (24 km) of attractive and fairly easy walking. An area has been set aside as a nature reserve managed by the Sussex Trust for Nature Conservation and great crested grebe, tufted duck, teal and widgeon, amongst others, are now breeding here. It is also an important staging post for migrating wildfowl.

Access to the reservoir, other than on foot, has been deliberately restricted, but at the main reception area there are excellent car-parking facilities, picnic areas and a visitor centre with informative displays. A reserved area of the car park gives the disabled visitor good views over the reservoir. Facilities are provided for trout fishing, sailing, rowing and canoeing, and there is a small steamboat which provides pleasant cruising on the reservoir (see page 110).

Blackdown, near Fernhurst (OS 186: SU 920293).

At 918 feet (280 metres), Blackdown is the highest point in Sussex. The dry acid soil gives typical heathland vegetation with heather and bracken, and some Scots pine and birch. On the eastern slopes are some fine beech trees and over 600 acres (240 hectares) of the area are now protected by the National Trust. Numerous paths and tracks cross the area; there is a nature trail and a footpath leads to the summit. There are excellent views over the Weald to the South Downs. High up on the east side is Aldworth House, built in 1869 as a summer residence for Alfred, Lord Tennyson, who spent the last twenty years of his life here.

Beachy Head, where the South Downs meet the English Channel.

Chichester Harbour

This is a huge expanse of semi-landlocked water of some 4000 acres (1600 hectares) and has been declared an Area of Outstanding Natural Beauty. An attractive area of open water, winding creeks, extensive saltings and mudflats, it is very popular for yachting and boating and is an important breeding ground for seabirds and waterfowl. On the eastern tip lies East Head, an area of active sand dunes, one of only three in Sussex.

Cuckoo Trail

This 10 mile (16 km) linear trail follows the route of the former railway line linking Polegate and Heathfield. The path is accessible to walkers, cyclists and horse riders and also to the disabled and runs through some very attractive countryside. Specially sculptured mileposts along the route were designed and made by local artists; each incorporates a hidden cuckoo in its design. A leaflet is available from local tourist information offices.

Ditchling Beacon (OS 198: TQ 333133). 1¹/₂ miles (2.5 km) south of Ditchling.

At 813 feet (246 metres), this is the third highest point on the South Downs. There are some good easy walks on the crest of the Downs along the South Downs Way and 2 miles (3 km) west lie the twin windmills of 'Jack' and 'Jill' at Clayton. The National Trust owns over 4 acres (1.6 hectares) of the north-facing scarp and adjoining is a reserve belonging to the Sussex Trust for Nature Conservation. The typical chalk grassland and flowers attract many insects including blue butterflies.

Traces of the ramparts and ditches of an iron age fort can be seen on the north scarp.

Ditchling Common Country Park (OS 198: TQ 336180). Just east of Burgess Hill at the intersection of B2113 and B2112.

This country park comprises nearly 200 acres (80 hectares) of old Weald clay common with developing woodland, established as a country park in 1974. The common supports a wide variety of birds, flowers and butterflies, many of which can be seen from the waymarked trail.

Downslink

This 30 mile (45 km) bridleway links the South Downs Way at Steyning, West Sussex, with the North Downs Way at St Martha's Hill in Surrey. Much of the route follows a disused railway track, providing a level waymarked route through some very attractive Wealden countryside and providing a haven for plants and wildlife. A leaflet is available from West Sussex County Council, County Hall, Chichester PO19 1RL, or local tourist information centres.

Fairlight Country Park (OS 199: TQ 860117). 3 miles (5 km) east of Hastings.

Between Hastings and Fairlight lie 5 miles (8 km) of unspoilt sandstone cliffs, split by glens covered in trees and gorse tumbling down to the sea. Over 540 acres (219 hectares), much of it declared an Area of Special Scientific Interest, were formed into a country park in 1974. The gorse-covered slopes are known as the Fire Hills from their fiery colour.

The Fairlight Clays form the lowest layer of the Hastings Beds and from the many fossil finds much of the ancient Wealden flora has been deduced. There are many footpaths through the park, including one to Hastings, but they are fairly steep going. There are also nature trails, with leaflets available from the interpretative centre, and access to the beach can be gained from Fairlight Glen. There are excellent views from the car park and a good picnic area.

Fairmile Bottom (OS 197: TQ 002108). 3 miles (4.5 km) north-west of Arundel.

Here are over 160 acres (64 hectares) of downland with open grassland and beech and yew woods. The flora and fauna are typical of the habitat. There are picnic areas and a waymarked trail.

Footland Wood (OS 199: TQ 763203). 4 miles (6 km) north of Battle.

Footland Wood appears in the Domesday Book of 1086, and in 1180 the Abbot of Battle appointed a professional forester to control the clearance of woodland.

The Forestry Commission acquired the derelict wood in 1934 and replanting continued until 1970, with a mixture of pine and beech. The wood was severely damaged in the hurricane-force winds of October 1987 but is being cleared and replanted. A waymarked forest trail leads from the picnic area and passes a small pond. The wood supports a variety of plant and animal life and over twenty species of bird have been recorded.

Foredown Tower Countryside Centre, Foredown Road, Hove. Telephone: 01273 422450.

Open: summer, daily; winter, Thursday to Sunday.

This former water tower, built in 1909, has been converted into a countryside centre and includes a camera obscura on the top which gives fascinating views over the downland and out to sea. There are other exhibits relating to the surrounding countryside and the tower is also the starting point for a number of circular walks.

Forest Way Country Park (OS 187: TQ 418357). 2 miles (3 km) south-east of East Grinstead.

This linear country park has been created along 9 miles (14 km) of disused railway line. The East Grinstead, Groombridge & Tunbridge Wells Railway opened in 1868 and closed almost a century later in 1967. The track has been removed and the path is suitable for walking and cycling through some peaceful countryside. Much of the track is suitable for pushchairs and invalid carriages. A good variety of flora and fauna inhabits the wayside and embankments.

Fore Wood, Crowhurst (OS 199: TQ 753128). 3 miles (5 km) south of Battle.

This large woodland reserve is owned by the Royal Society for the Protection of Birds and composed largely of broad-leaved trees, mainly oak. Several sandstone ravines cross the reserve and are rich in mosses and lichens. There are many bird species resident, including woodpeckers, nuthatches and tree-creepers.

Friston Forest. 6 miles (10 km) west of Eastbourne.

The forest extends over 2000 acres (800 hectares) of downland within the South Downs Area of Outstanding Natural Beauty. Planting began in 1926 and the aim has been to establish a mainly broad-leaved forest, principally beech. As it is only a mile (1.6 km) from the sea, salt-laden winds cause problems with cultivation, and pine was initially planted to protect the young beech. The pine is gradually being removed and by the late 1990s this should be one of the finest beech forests in southern England. The forest supports a wide variety of animals and plants, many of them found only on the chalk hills of the downland. The forest is well served by public footpaths and there are waymarked trails. There is a car park and picnic area adjacent to the Seven Sisters Country Park. On the northern boundary of the forest lies **Lullington Heath**, a National Nature Reserve. This is an unusual habitat known as chalk heathland, with sandy soil and chalk substrata; typical plants of heathland such as

gorse and heather occur side by side with deep-rooted chalk species. Entry to the reserve itself is by permit only.

Goodwood Country Park (OS 197: SU 898114). 6 miles (10 km) north-east of Chichester.

Opposite Goodwood Racecourse, the park covers over 60 acres (24 hectares) and was opened in 1971. The park is a mixture of woodland and typical downland grass, with walks, picnic areas and splendid views over the Coastal Plain to Chichester Harbour.

Kingley Vale (OS 197: SU 823105). 2¹/₂ miles (6 km) north of Chichester.

In 895 the Anglo-Saxon Chronicle says that marauding Vikings ravaged the Chichester countryside 'and the citizens put them to flight and killed many hundreds of them'. Local tradition says that the battle took place at Kingley Vale and that the superb grove of yew trees is descended from those planted on the graves of the dead. Whatever the truth of that, there is no doubting that the vale is filled with magnificent old yew trees and is the home of deer and badger and many birds and flowers. The reserve is managed by the Nature Conservancy Council and there is an information centre and a nature trail.

The Mens (OS 197: TQ 024237). 3 miles (5 km) north-east of Petworth.

This interesting area of Weald woodland is preserved by the Sussex Trust for Nature Conservation. There are many different trees and shrubs, including the wild service tree, and the area is rich in woodland flowers, birds, butterflies and various fungi and ferns.

Pagham Harbour (OS 197: SZ 856964). 5 miles (8 km) south of Chichester.

Over 1000 acres (400 hectares) of mud flats and saltings make this one of the best birdwatching areas of southern England, especially in spring and autumn. Over 260 species of bird have been recorded. Porpoises have been seen and occasionally seals approach the mouth. In the middle ages Pagham was a harbour but during severe storms in 1345 the sea flooded in; another attempt was made to create a harbour in the nineteenth century by building a sea wall, but in 1910 the sea again broke through and the attempt was abandoned. The reserve is managed by the West Sussex County Council and was declared a nature reserve in 1964. There is a waymarked trail and an information centre and there are numerous footpaths around the harbour. Visitors should note that the shingle bar is out of bounds during the breeding season.

Pulborough Brooks Nature Reserve, Wiggonholt, Pulborough (OS 197: TQ 060167). Telephone: 01798 875581. Royal Society for the Protection of Birds. *Open: daily.*

This RSPB reserve has nature trails and birdwatching hides around the attractive wetland area. There is a visitor centre with displays and also a tearoom.

Rye Harbour Nature Reserve (OS 189: TQ 930180). 2 miles (3 km) south of Rye.

This large expanse of shingle has been built up by the action of the sea, and an area of shingle beach and old gravel workings has been preserved as a local nature reserve. There are a number of public footpaths in the area and there are hides for birdwatching which are open to the public. The reserve is becoming an important wintering place for seabirds and there is a breeding colony of little terns. There is an information centre in the car park at the entrance to the reserve.

Seven Sisters Country Park (OS 199: TV 518996). 6 miles (10 km) west of Eastbourne. Telephone: 01323 870100.

Covering nearly 700 acres (280 hectares) of the Cuckmere valley, one of the few undeveloped river mouths on the south coast, the park extends from the A259 down to the sea on both sides of the meandering river Cuckmere and includes areas of bare chalk, shingle, open water, saltmarsh and meadow. The river mouth is flanked on either side by chalk cliffs, the Seven Sisters to the east and Seaford Head to the west. The park lies within a designated Area of Outstanding Natural Beauty and within the first stretch of British coastline to be recognised as a Heritage Coast,

the Sussex Heritage Coast from Seaford to Eastbourne.

There is a picnic area and car park adjacent to the A259 and a good information centre housed in an eighteenth-century flint barn in the former Exceat Farm. Another barn houses **The Living World**, an exhibition of living British and tropical insects and freshwater and marine life (open all year).

Slindon Estate (OS 197: SU 960080). 6 miles (10 km) north of Bognor Regis.

The estate, which once belonged to the Archbishops of Canterbury, is now in the care of the National Trust and covers over 3500 acres (1400 hectares) of unspoilt countryside. The park is a mixture of fine beech woods and farmland on the southern slopes of the Downs. Apart from the appeal of the landscape, Slindon is famous for its geological and historical remains. In palaeolithic times the sea came up to this point on the Downs and in the park a shingle beach can be seen, 130 feet (40 metres) above the present sea level, which escaped being covered with a chalk deposit. Other features are a $3^3/4$ mile (6 km) stretch of the Roman road Stane Street and numerous prehistoric barrows. A number of footpaths cross the park and there is free access to the public.

South Downs Way

This long-distance footpath runs for over 80 miles (129 km) from Eastbourne to Buriton in Hampshire, with an extension of some 20 miles (32 km) to Winchester. For much of the way the path keeps to the ridge of the Downs, giving some magnificent views and exhilarating walking. There is easy access to the path along much of its route.

Stoneywish Country Park, East End Lane, Ditchling (OS 198: TQ 337156). Telephone: 01273 843498. *Open: March to October, daily; November to February, weekends only.*

This former farm now provides an opportunity for visitors to see wildlife in its natural habitats. Along the trail are pieces of farm machinery, reminders of the former use of the land, and there are a number of ponds and

Littlehampton Beach.

lakes frequented by resident and migrating waterfowl. In the old farmyard is a pets' corner and a nineteenth-century flint barn has a display of photographs illustrating past life in the surrounding area. There are also tearooms and a picnic area.

Tilgate Forest Park, near Crawley (OS 187: TQ 275346).

This semi-formal park comprises over 400 acres (160 hectares) of fine Weald woodland, lakes and old hammer ponds on which ducks and grebes gather, especially in winter. There are sailing, canoeing and windsurfing on the larger of the lakes. It was in Tilgate Forest that Dr Gideon Mantell and his wife found the first remains of *Iguanodon*.

West Beach and Climping Beach (OS 197: TQ 006008).

The area between Littlehampton and Climping is the last undeveloped stretch of coastline in over 40 miles (60 km) of seafront from Brighton to Bognor Regis. All of the area is designated as either a nature reserve, a Site of Special Scientific Interest or a Site of Nature Conservation Importance. The low-water sandy beach is backed by shingle banks which in places bear vegetation, a rare habitat in Britain, and behind the shingle lie active sand dunes, another comparative rarity. Only six areas of active sand dunes exist on the entire south coast of England between Kent and Cornwall, three of them in Sussex. The area is an important habitat for many species of plants, insects and birds, particularly migrating ones. Over 230 species of plants, some local or national rarities, and over two hundred species of wild bird have been recorded here. A leaflet is available from: Project Officer, Arun District Council, Civic Centre, Maltravers Road, Littlehampton BN17 5LF (telephone: 01903 716133).

Woods Mill, Shoreham Road, Henfield (OS 198: TQ 218138). Telephone: 01273 492630. 1½ miles (3 km) south of Henfield.
Open: April to October, Saturdays, Sundays and bank holidays; also Tuesday to Thursday in school holidays.

This eighteenth-century mill is the headquarters of the Sussex Trust for Nature Conservation. The mill houses a wildlife and countryside exhibition which includes live animals such as harvest mice and fish from the lake in a large aquarium. There are two audio-visual programmes on 'Sussex Wildlife' and 'Sussex Nature Reserves' and a 25 feet (8 metres) tall model of an oak tree, installed in a stair well, which can be studied from roots to leaves. Surrounding the mill is a 15 acre (6 hectare) nature reserve with a good trail around woodland, marsh, streams and a lake. A particular attraction for children is a dipping pool where they may net and identify specimens; nets are provided.

4

Places of archaeological interest

For almost forty years from their discovery in 1912, the earliest humanoid remains were believed to be those of 'Piltdown Man'. Discovered by Charles Dawson, an amateur archaeologist from Lewes, they were hailed as the 'missing link' between man and ape. However, between 1949 and 1953, new techniques of dating revealed Piltdown Man to be a hoax! Until recently, the earliest evidence of man was restricted to flint implements and scrapings dating from the lower palaeolithic era and found at a number of sites, in particular Slindon. But in 1993 a bone fragment, dating from about half a million years ago, was found near Boxgrove and is believed to be from a direct ancestor of *Homo sapiens*. It is the earliest humanoid remain found so far in Britain and may be the earliest in Europe, suggesting that we may have to revise our estimate of the arrival of man's ancestors.

The mesolithic, or middle stone age, brought Neanderthal man, a nomadic hunter who roamed the Downs and Weald for some five or six thousand years but is not considered to be a direct ancestor of modern man. Large numbers of flint tools have been found from this period; at Selmeston, near Firle, over six thousand worked flints were found at one site.

The first settlement was by neolithic peoples from the continent and occurred around 3500 BC. They settled mainly on the downland areas of southern Britain and built five causewayed enclosures in Sussex. Neolithic man led an organised social life, carried out burials in impressive long barrows and mined flints for toolmaking. An adequate supply of flint for tools and weapons was important to stone age man. The usual method of mining was to dig down through the chalk until the flint layer was reached and then to drive radiating galleries along the seam of flint. Air supply limited the length of the galleries and when this limit was reached, or the seam ran out, another vertical shaft was dug. Many mines have been identified on the Downs, but the most important site was at Cissbury, which was second only to Grime's Graves in Norfolk as a centre for flint mining.

Settlement by the pastoral bronze age peoples began about 2000 BC. Many of their settlements were incorporated into later structures and many so-called iron age camps are bronze age in origin. This era is especially notable for the transition from mass burials in long barrows to individual burials in round barrows. These are very numerous on the Downs and over fifty can be seen in the vicinity of Firle Beacon (OS 198: TQ 485059). At Itford Hill (OS 198: TQ 435055) the relics of a bronze age field system and hamlet have been found. The hamlet contained thirteen circular timber-framed huts, and pottery finds indicate an occupation date of between 1000 and 750 BC.

By about 500 BC, farming communities were expanding through Sussex, and available farmland was becoming scarce. A new metal, iron, was being produced at various sites throughout the Weald. On the hilltops administrative and supply centres were constructed, with strong earthworks which seem to have been built to serve a more defensive purpose than the earlier causewayed enclosures.

Great changes occurred following the Roman invasion of AD 43. The leader of the Regni tribe of Sussex, Cogidubnus, became vassal king of Sussex. After subduing the other tribes, the Romans established their regional capital at Chichester, the only remaining Roman town in Sussex, and built roads and villas. Settlement was mainly to the west of the fort of *Anderida* at Pevensey and the east of the county seems to have been mainly concerned with the working of iron. Large quantities of slag, the waste product from the bloomeries, were found in the nineteenth century and very recent excavations suggest that the area north of Hastings may have been a collection and distribution area for the iron industry.

The following list is representative of the rich selection of pre-Norman sites which can be seen in Sussex.

Bignor Roman Villa, Bignor, Pulborough RH20 1PH (OS 197: SU 988147). Telephone: 01798 869259.

Open: March to May and October, Tuesday to Sunday and bank holiday Mondays; June to September, daily.

Discovered in 1811, these are the remains of one the largest villas found so far in Britain. Believed to date from the first century AD, the villa was of the courtyard type and enclosed an area of 4.5 acres (1.8 hectares). The inner courtyard measures 250 by 144 feet (76 by 44 metres) and the principal rooms of the north corridor contain some very fine mosaics depicting scenes of gladiators and representations of Venus and Medusa. One piece of mosaic, 80 feet (24 metres) long, is said to be the largest remaining intact in Britain.

Chanctonbury Ring, Washington (OS 198: TQ 139121).

The single bank of this iron age hillfort is probably the best-known landmark in Sussex because of the ring of beech trees which were planted in 1760 by Charles Goring, who lived at Wiston at the foot of the Downs. Set 783 feet (240 metres) up on the Downs, the 'ring' was very severely damaged by the hurricane-force winds which struck southern England on 16th October 1987. The trees have now been replanted but it will take some decades to achieve its former glory. Excavations in the interior in 1909 revealed the remains of a Romano-British temple dating from the first and second centuries AD. The root balls of the trees felled in the storm of 1987 brought up many other archaeological artefacts. John Galsworthy, who lived at nearby Bury, set the famous love scene between Fleur and Jon in *The Forsyte Saga* here.

Cissbury Ring, Worthing (OS 198: TQ 139080).

Two well-defined ramparts, enclosing an area of over 60 acres (24 hectares), make this the most impressive iron age fort on the South Downs. Dating from the third century BC, the defences were renewed in the late Roman period as a protection against Saxon raids. Excavations have revealed that the inner rampart, chiefly constructed of chalk rubble, was secured in front by nine to twelve thousand timber posts about 15 feet (4.5 metres) high. The site had obviously been occupied from a much earlier date, because within the perimeter of the fort are the remains of over two hundred neolithic flint mines. All of the mines have long since been filled in but are visible today as a series of shallow depressions.

Coombe Hill, Jevington (OS 199: TQ 575021).

This neolithic causewayed enclosure is 600 feet (200 metres) up on the Downs north-east of Jevington village. The enclosure consists of two concentric rings with internal banks.

Devil's Dyke, Poynings (OS 198: TQ 258111).

This natural formation of a deep dry valley is surmounted by an iron age promontory fort consisting of a single rampart with an external ditch. There is a road up to the fort, from where there are magnificent views; there is also a pub, but in Victorian times there was a cable car across the valley and a funicular railway from Brighton!

Fishbourne Roman Palace, Salthill Road, Fishbourne, Chichester PO19 3QR (OS 197: SU 838047). Telephone: 01243 785859. A Sussex Past property.

Open: mid February to mid December, daily; mid January to mid February, Sundays only.

The area around Fishbourne has long been known to have Roman connections, but only a few pieces of pottery had been found until 1960, when a workman uncovered part of this palace whilst digging a ditch. Sussex Archaeological Society (now known as Sussex Past) has extensively excavated and revealed the site of the largest Roman residence yet

Thirteenth-century fortifications at Pevensey Castle.

found in Britain. From its beginnings as a military base in AD 43, it developed into what was probably the palace of Cogidubnus and it was apparently destroyed by fire in about AD 280. The west and east wings have been excavated and reburied for their protection and the south wing probably lies under the A259. The north wing has been covered by a modern building, and raised walkways give a good idea of the ground plan and mosaics. The garden has been restored and planted with typical plants of the Roman period.

Highdown Hill, Ferring (OS 198: TQ 093043).

A single bank and ditch dating from the iron age about 500 BC enclose about 1.5 acres (0.6 hectare). Traces of a second bank of unknown date can be seen on the south side. Excavations revealed the post holes of an iron age hut, evidence of Romano-British occupation and a Saxon burial ground. The last contained eighty-six skeletons and several glass drinking vessels. In 1587 the site was used as a beacon to warn of the Spanish Armada and in the Second World War it was a radar station.

Holtye Common Roman Road (OS 188: TQ 463385). Access by footpath to the east of the White Horse inn on A264.

This well-preserved section of the London to Lewes road was excavated by I. D. Margery in 1939 and presented by him to the Sussex Archaeological Society. It varies in width from 14 to 20 feet (4 to 6 metres) and was built in the second century AD. Iron slag was used for the surface and it has rusted into a solid mass.

Hunter's Burgh, Arlington (OS 199: TQ 550036).

One of twelve neolithic long barrows on the South Downs, it was built of chalk about 2500 to 1800 BC as a burial chamber for the chiefs of local tribes and measures 190 by 75 feet (58 by 23 metres). Another example can be found below the crest of nearby Windover Hill at TQ 542033.

Long Man of Wilmington, Wilmington (OS 199: TQ 543035).

This impressive figure of a man, holding a staff in each hand, is some 227 feet (69 metres) high and is cut into the turf below Windover Hill. The figure has been carefully designed so as not to appear foreshortened when viewed from below. Although the earliest reference to it is only from the eighteenth century, nothing is known of its origins and it is believed to be much older. A good view of the figure can be had from the car park just south of Wilmington village on a minor road.

Mount Caburn, Glynde (OS 198: TQ 444089).

The defensive ramparts of this iron age hillfort are clearly defined; it occupies a splendid site overlooking the Ouse valley 1 to 1½ miles (1.6 to 2.4 km) from Lewes. Nearby are a number of clearly defined field systems and the single rampart of Ranscombe iron age camp.

Pevensey Castle, High Street, Pevensey (OS 199: TQ 645048). Telephone: 01323 762604. English Heritage.
Open: Easter to October, daily; November to Easter, Tuesday to Sunday.

This fortress, known as *Anderida* or *Anderita* to the Romans, was built in the fourth century AD as part of the defences against Saxon raiders. The walls, standing up to 30 feet (9 metres) in places, enclose an oval area of about 10 acres (4 hectares) and ten great bastions are spaced around the walls. Origi-

nally the sea covered what is now Pevensey Marshes and surrounded the castle on three sides. After the withdrawal of the Roman garrison, the fort was captured in AD 491 by the South Saxons led by Aella and Cissa, who killed all the inhabitants.

There are no records of subsequent occupation until the Norman invasion, when after the battle of Hastings a keep and bailey were built. In the thirteenth century an impressive stone curtain wall and gatehouse were added to the keep, but from then on, as the sea was pushed back by land reclamation, the military importance of the castle declined. The fort was briefly reoccupied, and new fortifications added, during the Spanish Armada scare in Tudor times and again during the Second World War. The castle now stands nearly 2 miles (3 km) from the sea.

The Trundle, Singleton (OS 197: SU 877111).

Overlooking Chichester and the Coastal Plain, this iron age hillfort dates from about 250 BC. The fort consists of a bank and ditch, with a lesser bank outside the ditch, and two of the original gateways. Within, and partly overlain by the ramparts, are the remains of a neolithic causewayed enclosure consisting of three concentric banks and ditches.

The coastal plain from the Trundle near Chichester.

5
Castles and fortifications

Sussex, with its long coastline and closeness to the continent, has for many centuries played a strategic role in Britain's defence. Almost every age has left its mark and examples from the Norman conquest to the Second World War can be seen.

Before the Norman Conquest in 1066 Sussex was divided into six areas called Rapes. William retained these as administrative areas, each protected by a strong castle, at Chichester, Arundel, Bramber, Lewes, Pevensey and Hastings.

The constant wars with France and French raids during the fourteenth century led to further fortifications and a number of royal licences were granted during this time to fortify manors or build castles. The castles at Amberley, Bodiam and Herstmonceux date from this period.

Following Henry VIII's break with Rome and the threat of invasion from Catholic powers, a series of castles was built from the Thames estuary to Cornwall; Camber is the only such castle in Sussex.

In the early part of the nineteenth century Britain was again at war with France and the threat of invasion brought a fresh spate of defence works on the Channel coast. These included the Royal Military Canal, the martello towers and larger forts at Eastbourne and Newhaven.

Amberley Castle, Amberley, near Arundel.
Not open to the public.

The castle was originally a manor house belonging to the Bishops of Chichester in the twelfth century. It was crenellated in 1377 by Bishop Rede to protect the nearby river Arun, then navigable to this point. The massive curtain wall on the north side rises from the marshes of Amberley Wild Brooks whilst, to the south, the main entrance is along a causeway with twin circular towers and a drawbridge over a dry moat. Inside, the Great Hall

dates from the fourteenth century. During the Civil War the castle was sacked; it was later reoccupied as a private residence and is now an hotel and restaurant.

Arundel Castle, Arundel BN18 9AB. Telephone: 01903 883136.
Open: April to October, Sunday to Friday; closed Good Friday.

Originally built by Roger de Montgomery in the eleventh century, Arundel Castle has for over four hundred years been the home of the Dukes of Norfolk, the hereditary Earls Marshal of England. During the Civil War, the castle was badly damaged by the Parliamentary forces under General Waller, and what is seen is largely a nineteenth-century reconstruction. The overall impression, however, is very striking, with its towers and battlements rising above the valley of the river Arun. Among the treasures is a fine collection of tapestries, furniture and paintings.

Bodiam Castle, Bodiam, near Robertsbridge. Telephone: 01580 830436. National Trust.
Open: mid February to October, daily; November to early January, Tuesday to Sunday.

Moated, picturesque and impressive, Bodiam presents the ideal picture of a castle. Square, with round towers at each corner and with strongly defended gateways, the massive curtain walls rise sheer from the moat. The castle was built in 1385 for comfort and defence. Like Amberley, it was designed to protect a then navigable river, in this case the Rother. Never used in anger, it was taken by Parliamentary forces in 1644, dismantled and left ruinous. In 1829 'Mad' Jack Fuller of Brightling (page 21) bought the castle to stop further damage, and later it was bought by Lord Curzon, who undertook extensive repairs and then bequeathed it to the National Trust. Little remains of the interior buildings, but much of the walls,

Bodiam Castle was built in 1387, when the technology of castle building was at its peak.

gatehouse and towers is accessible.

Bramber Castle, Bramber, near Steyning. National Trust.
Open at all reasonable times.

Bramber was built shortly after the Conquest by William de Braose to guard a then sizable port on the river Adur. Little remains except a fragment of the keep about 75 feet (24 metres) high and portions of the curtain wall. The mound on which the castle is built looks like a gigantic motte but it is natural and there is a pre-Conquest motte within the walls. From the site it can be seen what a very fine defensive position the castle occupied. During the Civil War the castle was attacked and destroyed by Parliamentary forces, who used the nearby church as a gun emplacement.

Camber Castle, near Winchelsea. Telephone Battle Abbey on 01424 775705 for information. English Heritage.
Open only by guided tours from Rye Heritage

Centre: Wednesdays, Fridays and Sundays, 10 a.m. and 2 p.m.

All the Henrican castles were designed to make good use of cannon. They are all symmetrical in plan with a pattern of lobes forming a series of gun platforms around a central tower. Their massive nature was designed to withstand enemy shot and they were essentially elaborate gun platforms with only basic accommodation. Traditional features such as moats, drawbridges and portcullises were included. Most were built in the 1540s but the first known fortification at Camber was built between 1512 and 1514. The main construction began in 1539 and was completed in 1544. Its purpose was to guard the river Rother, but the build-up of shingle made the castle useless and it was abandoned by 1640; it now lies over a mile from the sea. The castle has undergone extensive restoration and is now open to the public, by guided tour only, commencing from the Heritage Centre in Rye.

Chichester Castle, Chichester.
All that remains of this Norman castle is the motte.

Hastings Castle, Hastings. Telephone: 01424 717963.
Open: daily, but usually closed in January; telephone for times.
This was the first castle to be built after the Conquest. William had apparently already chosen the hill overlooking Hastings as the site for the prefabricated wooden fortress which he brought with him. After the success of the invasion, a stone castle was started in 1070 by Robert of Eu, who included a church of St Mary within the walls. The castle was enlarged and strengthened by the addition of a keep in the early 1170s by Henry II. Following the great storms of the thirteenth century which more or less finished Hastings as a major port, the castle fell into disrepair. Since then erosion of the cliffs has destroyed much of the site, so that only a segment of a once very large castle remains. Outside the walls, by the present entrance, is a series of narrow tunnels under the mound. They are called dungeons but were probably storerooms. Situated within the castle walls in a reconstruction of a medieval siege tent is **The 1066 Story**, a sound and light show which dramatically reconstructs the history of the castle and the battle of Hastings.

Herstmonceux Castle, Herstmonceux, near Hailsham BN27 1RP. Telephone: 01323 833816.
Grounds and gardens open: Easter to October, daily.
An especially beautiful castle, Herstmonceux is one of the earliest examples of a large brick building in Britain. It is believed that Flemish brickmakers were brought over to supervise the work. Built about fifty years later than Bodiam, in 1441, by Sir Roger de Fiennes, a veteran of Agincourt, it was much more a defended private house than a serious fortification. Apart from the high walls and the moat, the defences were concentrated in the fortified gateway, which was equipped with cannon; it was never attacked or besieged. In 1776 the interior was demolished to build nearby Herstmonceux Place and by Victorian times the castle was a 'romantic ruin'. Rebuilding and restoration were started in 1910 and in 1946 the castle became the home of the Royal Greenwich Observatory, which was forced to leave the smog of London. In 1987 government financial restrictions forced the relocation of the observatory to Cambridge University, bringing to an end over three hundred years as an independent observatory, the longest in the world. For some years the future of public access was in jeopardy as plans were put forward to turn the castle into an exclusive country club. However, in 1993 the castle and grounds were bought by Queen's University of Canada for an international study centre with guaranteed public access days to the gardens and grounds of over 200 acres (80 hectares).

Lewes Castle, Lewes. Telephone: 01273 486290. A Sussex Past property.
Open: daily.
Lewes Castle was built by William de Warrene in the eleventh century to defend the vital river crossing and must have been one of the strongest in England. The design is unusual in that, in addition to the normal motte and bailey, a second mound was built and each was surmounted by a shell keep, a plan not known anywhere else; only the south-western keep remains. In the thirteenth century two polygonal turrets were added to the existing keep and in the fourteenth century the southern gateway was fortified by the addition of 'the mightiest barbican in England', which still remains.
The castle was attacked only once, in 1264 during the battle of Lewes, when Simon de Montfort and his barons defeated Henry III and imposed conditions on the king which are regarded as the starting point of parliamentary democracy in England.

Martello towers
Over one hundred martello towers were built along the south coast between 1804 and 1810 as part of the coastal defence. They consist of a circular brick tower, with

Herstmonceux Castle was built in 1441.

a single first-floor entrance reached by re-movable steps. In some cases they were sur-rounded by a dry moat and reached by draw-bridge. Each had a garrison of over twenty men and had a single cannon on the roof. They are named after an ancient watchtower on Mortella Point in Corsica and numbered consecutively from east to west. By the time they were completed the fear of invasion had passed and not a single tower has fired a shot in anger. For a while the towers were used to accommodate the Coast Blockade, a forerunner of the present-day coastguard, and during the Second World War many of them were rearmed. Of forty-seven built in Sussex only eleven remain, the rest having been swept away by the sea or used for target practice.

Towers 28 and 30, Rye.

Number 28 lies just south of Rye Harbour, accessible by footpath. Number 30 can be seen at the side of the Winchelsea road just west of Rye. This was one of only two towers guarded by a wet moat. Both are on private property.

Tower 61, Martello Estate, Pevensey Bay.

The centrepiece of the estate just south of the A259, this tower clearly shows its brick construction. A further six towers can be seen from the beach between Langney Point and Norman's Bay. All are on private property.

Tower 73 (Wish Tower), King Edward's Parade, Eastbourne. Telephone: 01323 410440.
Open: April to September, daily.

This tower has been restored to show the details of construction and has displays giving the historical background to the period; it also houses the Coastal Defence Museum.

Martello Tower 74, The Esplanade, Seaford. Telephone: 01323 898222.
Open: Easter to October, Wednesdays, Saturdays, Sundays and bank holiday Mondays; November to Easter, Sundays.

This tower was built to supplement batteries at Seaford and Newhaven, to guard Seaford Bay and the harbour at Newhaven. It has been restored and now houses a museum of local history.

Newhaven Fort, Fort Road, Newhaven BN9 9DL. Telephone: 01273 517622.
Open: April to October, daily.

In 1859, with the threat of further French invasions, plans were made for a series of seventy-two coastal forts, including this one at Newhaven. Situated on a headland commanding a good field of fire, the massive walls and moat enclose an area of 10 acres (4 hectares). Within the wall is a central parade ground with perimeter casemates,

which provided quarters for the garrison of three hundred. The fort was sunk into the hillside, which is tunnelled with passageways and storerooms, now used as display rooms. The gun emplacements above the casemates housed forty-two guns. During the Second World War the armaments were updated but after the army left in 1956 the fort fell into disrepair. However, it has now been restored as a museum. There is a good adventure playground for children, a picnic area and a souvenir shop.

Pevensey Castle, Pevensey. See page 67.

Redoubt Fortress, Royal Parade, Eastbourne. Telephone: 01323 410300.
Open: Easter to October, daily.

This massive brick building was one of three built along the south coast to supplement the martello towers. It consists of two concentric brick walls sunk below ground level, surrounded by a dry moat and reached by a drawbridge. A ring of casemates, for stores and barracks, surrounded a central parade ground. Above the casemates is a platform to house eleven guns. The fortress now houses the Sussex Combined Services Museum.

Royal Military Canal

The canal was built in 1806 and runs for 30 miles (48 km) from Winchelsea to Hythe in Kent. A road was built behind it, the Royal Military Road, to allow rapid transport of troops and equipment and a gun turret was erected every quarter of a mile (400 metres). William Cobbett in *Rural Rides* was especially scathing about this defence work and wondered how a 30 feet (9 metres) wide ditch was to stop troops who had crossed the Rhine and Danube. It now provides pleasant walking and fishing along its banks.

6
Ecclesiastical buildings

Abbeys and priories

There were over thirty abbeys and priories in Sussex before the Dissolution of the Monasteries by Henry VIII in 1536. Of most of them little remains, but the few fragments which survive testify to the richness of building and decoration in them.

Battle Abbey, High Street, Battle TN33 0AE. Telephone: 01424 773792. English Heritage. *Open: daily.*

William the Conqueror vowed to build an abbey if given victory at the battle of Hastings. A church was built on the site of the battle and the high altar was situated on the spot where Harold fell. The abbey, which was probably completed before the Conqueror's death, was small, and little of the church remains. The monastic buildings were added to over the centuries and in 1338 the Abbot was given licence to crenellate. At that time the splendid gatehouse was built, but little building took place subsequently. After the Dissolution Henry VIII granted the abbey to his Master of Horse, Sir Anthony Browne, who, as one of the executors of the king's will, had the care of the young Princess Elizabeth. Having apparently pulled down the church almost at once, Sir Anthony set about incorporating some of the buildings into a house but he died before it was completed. The site of the battle, Senlac Field, is still open land and the view from the abbey remains over the battle ground is especially evocative. Some of the buildings are now occupied by a private school and are not open to the public.

Bayham Abbey, Lamberhurst TN8 8DE. Telephone: 01892 890381. English Heritage. Off B2169. *Open: April to September, daily.*

After Battle Abbey, these are the most extensive monastic ruins in Sussex. This small Premonstratensian abbey was built between 1208 and 1211 and apart from St Radegund's near Canterbury, in Kent, was the only abbey colonised directly from the mother house, the abbey of Prémonstré in France. The ruins stand in a peaceful valley by a lake formed by the little river Teise, which marks the boundary between Kent and Sussex; they make a picturesque scene. This was made use of by Humphry Repton in 1800 when planning the gardens of the mansion, also called Bayham Abbey, across the river in Kent.

Boxgrove Priory, Boxgrove. 4 miles (6 km) east of Chichester.

Boxgrove was a Benedictine priory founded in 1115 on land given to the abbey of Lessay in Normandy by Robert de Mortain, to mark his marriage to the daughter of the Earl of Arundel. Little remains of the monastic buildings except part of the priory church, which is now the parish church. The secular and clerical portions of the building were separate and after the Dissolution the parochial nave was demolished and the parish then had the use of the rest of the church. The choir, transepts and a small part of the nave of the original building remain and are very attractive. The chancel is, after Chichester Cathedral, the most important Early English style building in the county. There is a very fine monument to the ninth Lord De La Warr, built in 1526, and on the ceiling of the choir are paintings by Lambert Barnard, who died around 1567.

Easebourne Priory, Easebourne, near Midhurst. On A272.

What remains of Easebourne Priory is now incorporated in the present vicarage and church of St Mary and consists of two sides of the building around the cloisters. The priory of Augustinian nuns was founded here before 1238 as part of an endowment to the abbey of

The ruins of a Premonstratensian foundation, Bayham Abbey, stand close to the border with Kent.

Seez in Normandy. The canonesses did not build their own church but made use of the parish church. This dates from the twelfth century but, apart from the tower, was much overrestored in 1869. Village legends suggest that some of the nuns were not as pious as they should have been and used to meet local bachelors in secret at a house in Easebourne Street called Bachelors' Gate, which is still in existence.

Lewes Priory, Southover, Lewes.

Little more than the foundations remain of the priory of St Pancras which was founded in 1077 by William de Warrenne and his wife Gundrada. The only Cluniac monastery in Sussex, this was the greatest house of its order in England and at one time held fifty-six churches in the county. At the Dissolution the king's commissioner, Thomas Cromwell, employed an Italian engineer to destroy it and many churches in Sussex incorporated parts

of the masonry and carvings in their fabric. What remained was further damaged in 1845, when the railway line to Brighton was laid through the site. During the work, the tombs of the founders, William and Gundrada, were discovered and the interest generated by that led, in 1846, to the foundation of the Sussex Archaeological Society. In 1847 a neo-Norman chapel was built on the south side of St John's church in Southover High Street to house the remains, and parts of the original tomb furnishings, which had been removed to Isfield church, were returned. The remains of the priory are fenced but can be clearly seen.

Michelham Priory, Upper Dicker, Hailsham BN27 3QS. Telephone: 01323 844224. A Sussex Past property.
Open: late March to October, daily; rest of March and November, Sundays.

Set on a moated island in a bend of the river Cuckmere and surrounded by spacious gardens, the priory was founded in 1229 by Gilbert de l'Aigle for Augustinian canons. Approached through a fourteenth-century gatehouse, over a sixteenth-century bridge spanning the longest medieval moat in England, most of the original buildings were demolished at the Dissolution by Henry VIII, but the remains evolved into a Tudor farm and splendid country house that now contains a fascinating array of exhibits. Outside, the picturesque gardens are enhanced by a watermill (see page 108), physic garden, smithy, rope museum and the dramatic Elizabethan Great Barn.

Robertsbridge Abbey, Robertsbridge. 1 mile (1.6 km) east of village off A21.
The remains are occasionally open to the public.
Little remains of this, the only Cistercian monastery in Sussex. Aerial photographs have revealed the outline of a church 210 feet (70 metres) long, half as large again as the parish church at Salehurst across the river. Nothing is visible now except parts of the refectory

The fourteenth-century gateway at Michelham Priory.

and the abbot's house, built about 1225 and incorporated into a private dwelling. There is an impressive west window which is visible from the road and a vaulted undercroft and thirteenth-century roof.

Wilmington Priory, Wilmington, Polegate BN26 5SW.
Currently closed to the public, but much of it is visible from the road or the nearby public car park.
The priory was founded before 1100 for the Benedictine abbey of Grestain in Normandy, but much of the present building dates from the fourteenth century. It rarely had more than two or three monks in residence and they used the parish church rather than build their own establishment. Their chief occupation was the oversight of the abbey's various English estates and the collection of rents.

Churches and meeting houses

Sussex is rich in parish churches and almost every village has a church which dates in part from Norman times or earlier. Some that are of special interest are described in this section.

Ashburnham: St Peter. (Off A271 west of Battle.)
The exterior of this church looks to be all from the fourteenth century, but only the west tower is original: the rest dates from the rebuilding in 1665 by John Ashburnham. There are some fine interior features including panelled wagon roofs and an organ gallery across the west end of the nave which is reached by an attractive wooden staircase. The church is built on the Ashburnham Estate, now a Christian trust, and there are a number of monuments to the Ashburnham family, including one to John Ashburnham, the builder, lying between his two wives, and another to William, his brother, kneeling before his dying wife. The grandfather of these two was Groom of the Bedchamber to Charles I and for many years the church had on display a number of relics of the king, including a shirt worn by him at his execution, but they are no longer there.

Ashurst: St James. (On B2135 4 miles, 6 km, north of Steyning.)

This small church lies at the edge of the village in remote, quiet farmland. It is built of flint, and parts are roofed with Horsham slate. It dates mainly from the twelfth century, but parts are probably older. Inside there is much good timber work, with a king-post roof spanning the nave and aisles and a simple oak beam in place of an arch between nave and chancel. Margaret Fairless Barber (died 1901), who wrote the 'Roadmender' stories under the pen-name Michael Fairless, is buried in the churchyard.

Berwick: dedication unknown. (Off A27 east of Lewes.)

Flint, with a shingled broach spire, this small fourteenth-century church sits at the foot of the north face of the Downs. Its chief interest is the series of wall paintings by Duncan Grant and Vanessa and Quentin Bell, who lived nearby at Charleston Farmhouse (see page 83). They were commissioned by Bishop Bell of Chichester in 1943 and many local people were used as models.

Bishopstone: St Andrew. (Off A259 northwest of Seaford.)

This lovely church, set against the backdrop of the Downs, incorporates some of the earliest Saxon work in Sussex. The present porch was originally a side chamber and, together with much of the nave, probably dates from the ninth century. The Normans added much to the church in the twelfth century, including the west tower, which is built in four stages, and the chancel. A very fine doorway with chevron mouldings was inserted in the porch. Other items of interest are a Saxon sundial above the doorway and a twelfth-century coffin lid in the south wall of the tower.

Blue Idol Meeting House, Coolham, near Billingshurst.

This seventeenth-century timber-framed farmhouse was converted into a Quaker meeting house for William Penn in 1691. One end of the building had the first-floor timbers removed to produce a galleried room. Penn lived at Warminghurst, about 4 miles (6 km) away, and walked here for meetings. The origin of the name is uncertain but the generally accepted one is that when the meeting house was 'idle' or unused during the nineteenth century it was colour-washed in blue and thus became the 'blue idle meeting house'! It is now simply white and in use again as a Friends' meeting house.

Burpham: St Mary the Virgin. (3 miles, 5 km, north-west of Arundel on minor road.)

This impressive-looking cruciform church is mostly Norman with the addition of the fourteenth-century west tower. It was carefully restored in 1868. The vaulted chancel, with zigzag and chevron mouldings and carvings of foliage and grotesque heads, is particularly attractive. Of particular note are the two piscinas and the double aumbry.

Chichester Cathedral

The centre of the early Christian church in Sussex was at Selsey, where St Wilfrid founded his church, but in 1080 the Norman centralisation of sees established the cathedral in Chichester on the site of a Saxon church.

The first cathedral was small but a new one was started by Bishop Luffa in 1091 and consecrated by Bishop Seffrid in 1184. It is this church, Norman in design, which forms the main body of the present cathedral. Two towers flank the west door and to the north lies the detached bell-tower, built in the fourteenth century to relieve the pressure on the central tower. A fire in 1187 destroyed the wooden roof and clerestory and these were rebuilt and stone vaulting was added to the roof; external buttresses were added to take the increased thrust. At this time the retrochoir, one of the most attractive features of the cathedral, was built in Early English style. In the retrochoir is a modern altar on the site of the shrine to Bishop Richard de Wych, 1245–53, who was canonised in 1262 and became an object of pilgrimage to rival St Thomas à Becket at Canterbury.

Later in the thirteenth century a series of chapels flanking the nave aisles was built and the exterior walls were pierced, producing a double aisle which gives an open feel to the interior. Further additions were made over the next three hundred years in both the Decorated and Perpendicular styles.

In the fourteenth century the first spire was added to the central crossing tower. The present spire, 265 feet (82 metres) high, is the only English cathedral spire visible from the sea. It was repaired in the seventeenth century by Sir Christopher Wren, was struck by lightning in 1721 and collapsed completely in 1861. It was subsequently rebuilt by Sir George Gilbert Scott and over the last decade or so has undergone extensive repairs, but finally in 1992 the scaffolding was removed, allowing the cathedral to be seen in full again.

In 1860, fortuitously in view of the collapse of the spire in the following year, a fifteenth-century Perpendicular-style stone screen, known as the Arundel Screen, was removed from its position between nave and chancel and stored in the campanile. In 1960 it was restored to its original position in memory of Bishop Bell.

There are numerous monuments of interest, including a fine one to Richard Fitzalan, fourteenth Earl of Arundel, and his wife and one to William Huskisson, MP for Chiches-ter, who had the dubious distinction of being the first person in England to be killed in a railway accident. Attending the opening of the Liverpool & Manchester Railway in 1830, he was knocked down by a train and died later from his injuries.

The cathedral was badly damaged in the Civil War and no original glass survives but there is some interesting modern work including a window by Marc Chagall. The Great Window in the south transept was restored in 1932 and the corbel table above was refashioned in the likenesses of contemporary figures such as King George V, Ramsey MacDonald, Stanley Baldwin and others. There are some paintings by the sixteenth-century artist Lambert Barnard and modern works by Graham Sutherland amongst others. A striking feature of the high altar is the modern reredos installed in 1966 which takes the form of a tapestry designed by John Piper and woven in Aubusson, France. Two items of especial interest are the sculptured panels in the south aisle which may date from as early as the year 1000.

Chichester is not one the greatest of the English cathedrals but it is in close contact with its city and has a very homely feel to it.

The Fitzalan monument in Chichester Cathedral.

There are none of the usual domestic buildings associated with monastic foundations, but there is a fifteenth-century cloister, with attractive wooden barrel vaulting, and a bishop's palace which dates in part from the original work of Bishop Seffrid.

Clayton: St John the Baptist. (2½ miles, 4 km, south-west of Ditchling on A273.)

The exterior of this simple village church nestling at the foot of the Downs gives no clue as to the quality of the interior. The chancel is largely nineteenth-century, but much of the rest is Saxon work. However, the thing that strikes one first is the wall paintings which cover much of the nave. They date from about 1140 and were probably done by artists from St Pancras Priory in Lewes.

Climping: St Mary. (2 miles, 3.5 km, west of Littlehampton, north of A259.)

The impression one gets of the solid tower of this village church is of a Norman keep

The fortress-like tower of Climping church.

and, in an unsettled age, perhaps it was designed to serve a dual function. It dates from about 1220, although the lower part is older, and was built, in Caen stone, by John de Climping, who became Bishop of Chichester in 1253. The beautiful doorway has deep moulding and dog-tooth and zigzag decoration and on three sides of the tower are central buttresses pierced by windows with equally fine decorations and said to be unique in England. On the south face of the tower are a number of 'mass dials', simple sundials operated by inserting a stick in the central hole and indicating the next mass. The interior is very attractive with a fine arcade of thirteenth-century Early English style arches between the nave and south aisle and over the chancel and transepts. There is a thirteenth-century piscina and a crusaders' chest for offerings for poor knights to go to the Crusades. Parts of the fourteenth-century pews also remain.

'Climping for perfection' is an old Sussex saying, and the church certainly lives up to it.

Etchingham: St Mary and St Nicholas. (11 miles, 18 km, north-east of Heathfield, on A285.)

This solid-looking church with its massive central tower dates entirely from its rebuilding in 1366 by William de Etchingham and is the finest example of Decorated work in Sussex. The church is unusual in that the nave is shorter than the chancel, but this is because it was a collegiate foundation rather than a parish church. The choir stalls are contemporary with the church and there are some very fine misericords. There are also some good brasses and fourteenth-century tiles. One of the monuments is to Henry Corbould, the designer of the 'Penny Black', the world's first postage stamp. Outside, the beautiful tracery of the windows is especially obvious and on the tower is perhaps the oldest weathervane in Britain, contemporary with the building. A representation of the de Etchingham coat of arms, the design was used by the Post Office as a cancellation stamp for commemorative stamps issued in 1990, 150 years after the introduction of the 'Penny Black'.

Etchingham church is the finest example of Decorated architecture in Sussex.

Ford: St Andrew. (North-west of Little-hampton, between A27 and A259.)

Lying isolated in fields by the side of the river Arun, this tiny flint church, dating from the eleventh century, is one of the prettiest in Sussex. An attractive white weatherboarded bellcote was added in the nineteenth century and an elegant brick porch dates from 1637.

Glynde: St Mary. (North of A27, south-east of Lewes.)

With the exception of nonconformist chapels, not much church building took place in Sussex between the Dissolution of the Monasteries and the frenzy of activity in Victorian times. A Palladian-style church is therefore something of a rarity. Built by Bishop Trevor of Durham, who inherited Glynde Place, this is a fine example built of knapped, squared flint with an ashlar porch and other features. The interior is very pleasant, not overrestored, and there is a good Venetian window, some box pews and an attractive staircase leading to the gallery. In the churchyard are some terracotta tomb plaques by Jonathan Harmer.

Hardham: St Botolph. (Just south of Pulborough, on A29.)

This small unspoilt village church dates mainly from the eleventh century with the additions of a few windows in the fourteenth century and a Victorian bell turret. The interior consists of a small nave and chancel and there is a good king-post roof. The main feature is the remains of wall paintings, badly faded, over much of the nave and chancel. They date from the twelfth century and were done by artists from the Priory of St Pancras at Lewes.

Herstmonceux: All Saints. (East of Hailsham, off A271.)

The church lies at the gates to Herstmonceux Castle overlooking the Pevensey Marshes and well away from the present village centre. A church existed on the site at Domesday, but the earliest part now evident is the north-west tower dating from the twelfth century. There are also additions from the fourteenth century in Decorated style and some not very good Victorian restoration. Inside, there is a fine brass of Sir William Fiennes (died 1402), the father of the castle builder, and a very attractive canopied monument believed to be to Lord Dacre, who died in 1533, and his son, who died earlier. However, it appears that the monument was originally for Thomas, Lord Hoo (died 1455), and his half-brother Sir Thomas Hoo and was brought from Battle Abbey at the Dissolution and reused!

Lullington: dedication unknown. (In the Cuckmere valley, north-east of Seaford.)

This tiny church, only 16 feet (5 metres) square, is claimed to be the smallest in England but it is only the chancel of a once much larger church, the nave having fallen down long ago. It dates from the twelfth century or earlier, but its chief attraction is its isolated position amongst the Downs. It overlooks Alfriston and the river Cuckmere and is reached by footpath from the village. Sir Dirk Bogarde, the actor, describes visits to the church in his delightful childhood autobiographies, *A Postillion Struck by Lightning* and *Great Meadow*.

North Marden: St Mary. (North-west of Chichester on B2141.)

Small and remote, the church of St Mary is approached through a farmyard. It represents one of the simplest of Norman buildings; nave and chancel are continuous, with an apsidal chancel. It dates from the mid twelfth century; the porch is a later addition but a very fine doorway is original and is made of Caen stone. In the apse, only one of the windows is original, the other two being very good copies. The nearby villages of East Marden and Up Marden also have very fine Norman churches.

Penhurst: St Michael. (6 miles, 10 km, west of Battle, off A271.)

This small fourteenth-century church is chiefly memorable for its position. It lies amidst farmland and woodland and the name means 'head of the wood'. Penhurst is an example of a manorial group, with the church lying side by side with a small Elizabethan manor farmhouse and farm buildings. The pond in front of the group may be the remains of a moat which surrounded the site. In the Domesday Book Penhurst was recorded as having 'two villeins with two ploughs and one acre of meadow and wood for two hogs';

it seems hardly bigger now.

Piddinghoe: St John. (Just north of Newhaven, in the Ouse valley.)

The unusual tower of this flint church is one of only three round towers in Sussex. The two others are also in the Ouse valley, at Southease and St Michael's, Lewes. Several theories have been put forward for the round towers: it was cheaper to build as no quoin stones were needed; they may have been watch-towers; or they may have been distinctive navigation marks. We shall probably never know. Parts of the church are Norman but it was restored in 1882. Hard on the bank of the river, the roof on the river side comes down very low, which is an acknowledgement of the windiness of the site. Kipling, in his poem 'Sussex', makes reference to this: 'South where windy Piddinghoe's begilded dolphin veers'. The dolphin refers to the gilded weathervane, which is actually a sea-salmon, but that does not scan as well.

Shoreham-by-Sea: St Mary de Hadura, New Shoreham.

Shoreham is one of the few places to have two Norman churches. New Shoreham was planned about 1110 to overcome the problems of silting in the harbour and the building of the church seems to have started in 1103, before the rebuilding at Old Shoreham. Building continued for over a century, spanning the architectural periods between Norman and Gothic. The present church is only half its original length; much of the nave fell down in 1700, perhaps as the result of a great storm which caused other damage in the town, and was finally demolished and blocked up in 1720. What remains is very impressive with its 80 feet (25 metres) high tower and the Early English style flying buttresses on each side of the choir. The interior has some very fine arcading, with examples of both Norman and Transitional style arches and carvings.

Shoreham-by-Sea: St Nicholas, Old Shoreham.

The earlier church, St Nicholas at Old

Opposite: Chichester Cathedral.

Shoreham, was originally Saxon and still retains some features from this period. The rebuilding of the church started in about 1140 with the development of a cruciform church with a central tower. In about 1300 the chancel was rebuilt in Early English style but the interior is dominated by the fine Norman arches on the four sides of the tower crossing.

Slindon: St Mary. (North of Bognor Regis, off A29.)

The church is partly Norman, although much overrestored, but is worth a visit for the monument to Sir Anthony St Leger (died 1539), the only wooden effigy in Sussex.

Sompting: St Mary. (Just north of Worthing, by the A27.)

The important feature of this church is its Saxon tower with the so-called 'Rhenish helm' gabled cap, common in the Rhine area of Germany but now unique in England. The gables are covered in oak shingles and inside the spire are the original Saxon timbers. Inside the tower, the nave arch is an important example of Saxon architecture. In 1154 the church was granted to the Knights Templars, who rebuilt the nave and chancel. The church is a distinctive landmark at the side of the A27. Although once some way removed from Sompting village, it is now gradually becoming surrounded by development.

Twineham: St Peter. (West of A23, west of Burgess Hill.)

In a very isolated position, Twineham church is unusual in being built entirely of brick; it dates from the early Tudor period. The tower has a low shingled spire and the roof is covered with Horsham slates. Of interest inside are the tower gallery and the Jacobean family pews. One part of the churchyard was given over to Quakers from 1694 to 1732, a most unusual arrangement.

Worth: St Nicholas. (Just east of Crawley.)

This is the finest example of a Saxon church in Sussex. Built on a cruciform plan with an apsidal chancel, it dates largely from the tenth century, although there was some restoration in the mid nineteenth century, including the building of the Norman-looking north-east tower in 1871 by Anthony Salvin. From the outside, the main Saxon features visible are the three windows in the nave formed by twin arches separated by a stone baluster and the vertical pilaster strips which divide the masonry of the walls into bays and are a feature of late Saxon work. The twin-arched windows in the apse are Victorian. Inside, the Saxon work is more striking. Cruciform churches from this period were rarely formed by a central tower and the transepts were, as here, more like side chapels. The arches to these transeptal chapels and the chancel are very fine Saxon work. Various additions have been made over the centuries but the basic Saxon origins of this lovely church are still very apparent.

7
Historic houses and gardens

Bateman's, Burwash, Etchingham TN19 7DS. Telephone: 01435 882302. National Trust.
Open: April to October, Saturday to Wednesday.
Originally built for a Sussex ironmaster in 1634, in one of the Weald's most attractive valleys, Bateman's was the home of Rudyard Kipling from 1902 until his death in 1936. Kipling's love of the Orient is reflected in the silk embroidery, porcelain and bronzes, but the furniture is mainly seventeenth-century English. He wrote many of his books here, including *Puck of Pook's Hill*, the hill itself being visible from the study window. The study has been preserved as it was during Kipling's lifetime. The enclosed gardens, designed by the Kiplings, run down to the river Dudwell, where a watermill still stands and grinds corn and where a water turbine was installed by Kipling to provide electricity for the house (see page 105).

Borde Hill Garden, Haywards Heath RH16 1XP. Telephone: 01444 450326.
Open: April to October, daily.
This large garden has an excellent collection of rare shrubs and trees, azaleas and rhododendrons and is particularly attractive in spring and early summer. The collection was started in the early 1890s by Colonel Stephenson Clarke and has been continued by successive members of the family. There are splendid views over the Weald, as well as a woodland walk and a picnic area.

Brickwall House and Garden, Northiam, Rye TN31 6NJ. Telephone: 01797 252494 or 223329 (curator).
Open: April to September, Saturdays and bank holiday Mondays.

This attractive timber-framed Jacobean house has been the home of the Frewen family since 1666 and contains family portraits spanning the centuries. There are some especially fine seventeenth-century plaster ceilings and staircases. The grounds include formal gardens, a topiary chess garden, an arboretum and a picnic area.

Charleston Farmhouse, Firle, Lewes BN8 6LL. Telephone: 01323 811265 (visitor information).
Open: April to October, Wednesday to Sunday and bank holiday Mondays.
This pretty farmhouse dating from the seventeenth or eighteenth century was the home from 1916 of Vanessa and Clive Bell and Duncan Grant. Decorated by the artists in characteristic Bloomsbury style, both house and garden, where the best-known intellectuals and artists of the day were frequent visitors, are particularly evocative of the period.

Danny, Hurstpierpoint, Hassocks BN6 9BB. Telephone: 01273 833000.
Open: May to September, Wednesdays and Thursdays.
This splendid Elizabethan house, standing in extensive grounds at the foot of the Downs, dates from about 1580 and incorporates part of a medieval farmhouse. The main front is of the classic E shape of Tudor times, with tall mullioned windows.
In the eighteenth century a Queen Anne style façade was added to the south, and the house now has the unusual feature of two 'fronts' dating from distinct architectural periods. Inside, a ceiling was added to the original open timbers of the Great Hall, which can still be seen above the ceiling. During the First World War the house was let to the

Bateman's, the home of Rudyard Kipling.

Prime Minister, David Lloyd George, and the terms of the Armistice were drawn up by the War Cabinet in the Great Hall. The name Danny is a corruption of the Saxon *Daneghithe*, which means a valley and haven.

Denmans, Fontwell, near Arundel BN18 0SU. Telephone: 01243 542808.
Open: daily.
   This attractive garden is the creation, over forty years, of the present owners. There are a variety of environments including a walled garden, a gravelled area and water gardens which provide plenty of year-round interest. A former greenhouse has been utilised to contain unusual tender plants.

Firle Place, Firle, Lewes BN8 6LP. Telephone: 01273 858335.
Open: May to September, Wednesdays, Thursdays and Sundays; also Easter, Spring and August bank holiday Sundays and Mondays.
   Attractively situated at the foot of the Downs, Firle Place has been the home of the Gage family for more than five hundred years,

having been built by Sir John Gage, who was Vice-Chamberlain to Henry VIII and Captain of the Royal Guard. The original house was incorporated into the present house, which was remodelled by Sir Thomas Gage in 1745. The Great Hall is that of the Tudor house, and above the ceiling the original hammerbeam roof is still in existence. General Sir Thomas Gage was Commander-in-Chief of the British forces at the beginning of the American War of Independence and was defeated by the Americans at Bunker Hill. His son became the third Viscount. There is a remarkable collection of European and English old master paintings, some fine English and French furniture and notable Sèvres porcelain. Also of interest is an early seventeenth-century map of New York on which Wall Street is clearly shown, running behind the city walls!

Glynde Place, Glynde, Lewes BN8 6SX. Telephone: 01273 858224.
Open: May to September, Wednesdays, Thursdays and Sundays; also Easter and bank holiday Mondays.
   An attractive flint building dating from

Glynde Place and church.

1570, Glynde Place was built for William Morley on the site of an earlier house. A descendant of William Morley, Harbart Morley, was one of the judges at the trial of Charles I but refused to sign the death warrant and was thus able to buy his pardon at the Restoration. In 1743 Bishop Richard Trevor inherited the estate and remodelled the interior along classical lines but left the exterior, apart from a new entrance created on the east side. The house is now approached through the stables, which were built in 1760. Beside the gateway is the parish church, built in 1763–5 in Palladian style (see page 79). The house contains a good collection of paintings, bronzes and historical documents, including a room dedicated to Mr Speaker Brand (1874–82). Around the house are terraces and formal gardens, protected from grazing cattle by a ha-ha.

Goodwood House, Chichester PO18 0PX. Telephone: 01243 774107.
Open: Easter Sunday and Monday; then May to September, Sunday and Monday; also Tuesdays, Wednesdays and Thursdays in August.

Closed on days of horse-racing at Goodwood.
The ancestral home of the Dukes of Richmond, the original house was built for the first Duke, who was the son of Charles II and his French mistress, Louise de Querouaille. The present large house incorporates the earlier one and was built for the third Duke by James Wyatt in 1790. The central porticoed wing and the two side wings represent the first stages of a large octagon, but the money ran out before completion! The house contains a good collection of paintings, including Van Dyck, Reynolds, Stubbs and Canaletto, some superb eighteenth-century furniture and a good collection of Sèvres porcelain and Gobelin tapestries.

Great Dixter, Northiam, Rye TN31 6PH. Telephone: 01797 252878.
Open: April to October, Tuesday to Sunday.
This fine Wealden hall-house was built about 1450 and was in a tumbledown state when bought by the Lloyd family in 1910. Sir Edwin Lutyens was employed to restore the house, and he added a small extension to the side and, at the rear, another complete timber-

framed house from Benenden in Kent. The restoration was done with great sensitivity and the Great Hall, with its solar above, is a magnificent room. The gardens, also designed by Lutyens, are particularly attractive, with a series of small gardens around the original farm buildings.

The Lloyd family still owns the house, and the gardens are now under the care of Christopher Lloyd, the gardening writer.

Hammerwood, near East Grinstead RH19 3QE. Telephone: 01342 850594.
Open: Easter Monday to September, Wednesdays, Saturdays and bank holidays.

Built in 1792, Hammerwood was the first commission for the young architect Benjamin Latrobe. He built only one other house in England before emigrating to the United States, where he was to build the Capitol Building in Washington DC, redesign the White House and design Baltimore Cathedral, amongst other works. Restoration of the derelict house, terraces and water gardens started in 1982 and the owner's enthusiasm continues unabated.

Haremere Hall, Etchingham TN19 7QJ. Telephone: 01580 812245.
Open: April to October, daily.

This large symmetrical Jacobean house dates from the early part of the seventeenth century and stands on high ground overlooking the Rother valley. There are attractive terraced gardens, and the heavy working horses which have been reintroduced to the estate are a big attraction. Shires, French Ardennes and Welsh cobs are being integrated into the farming and forestry operations of the estate.

High Beeches, Handcross RH17 6HQ. Telephone: 01444 400589.
Open: Easter to June and September to October, daily except Wednesdays.

These 20 acres (8 hectares) of landscaped woodland gardens form one of the best spring gardens in the county. Rhododendrons, azaleas and camellias are interspersed amongst a sea of daffodils and bluebells and there is a wildflower meadow. Autumn provides an-

other spectacular show of colour from the maples, nyssas and liquidambars.

Highdown Gardens, Goring-by-Sea, Worthing BN12 6PE. Telephone: 01903 501054.
Open: April to September, daily; October to March, Monday to Friday.

This 9 acre (3.6 hectare) garden was started in 1909 by Sir Frederick Stern in a disused chalk pit. Despite expert predictions that 'nothing would ever grow there', by the time of Sir Frederick's death in 1967 the garden had become famous for its collection of lime-loving plants. In springtime the garden is particularly pretty with rafts of daffodils, crocuses and other spring flowers.

Kidbrooke Park, Forest Row. Telephone: 01342 822275. 1 mile (1.6 km) south of Forest Row off A22.
Open: Spring Bank Holiday Monday and daily during August.

This attractive sandstone house was originally built in 1724 for Lord Abergavenny but was added to in Victorian times. It was for some time the home of Charles Abbot, Lord Colchester, who was Speaker of the House of Commons from 1802 to 1817. The house, situated on the edge of Ashdown Forest, is now used as a school and the interior is not open to the public, but the park, which was landscaped by Humphry Repton, is. There are fine views over the surrounding countryside and there are terraces, pergolas, ponds and a wild garden.

Lamb House, West Street, Rye TN31 7ES. Telephone enquiries: 01892 890651. National Trust.
Open: April to October, Wednesdays and Saturdays.

The house was originally built in 1723 for James Lamb, who became mayor in the same year. He subsequently served as mayor thirteen times and his son held the office for twenty terms! In 1899 the house was bought by Henry James, the American novelist, who spent the last eighteen years of his life here. There is a small collection of the personal belongings of James and a large garden which he enjoyed. The house was later

Haremere Hall is a handsome Jacobean house overlooking the Rother valley.

the home of the author Edward Frederic Benson (1867–1940).

Leonardslee Gardens, Lower Beeding, Horsham RH13 6PP. Telephone: 01403 891212.
Open: April to October, daily.

The 240 acre (100 hectare) valley at Leonardslee Gardens is world-famous for its spring display of rhododendrons and azaleas. Largely created by Sir Edmund Loder from 1889, it is now one of the most spectacular woodland gardens in England. The paths wind down the valley sides through the almost tropical scenery and around the seven lakes. Leonardslee is at its best in May when the rock garden is a kaleidoscope of colour and the fragrance of the huge blooms of *Rhododendron loderi* pervades the air. The new wildflower walk in summer and the vivid autumn tints from maples and hickories complete the seasons. The bonsai exhibition shows this fascinating living art-form to perfection. The alpine house has four hundred alpine plants in a natural rocky setting. Wallabies have lived wild in part of the garden for over one hundred years, and deer may be seen in the parks.

Monk's House, Rodmell, Lewes BN7 3HF. Telephone enquiries: 01892 890651. National Trust.
Open: April to October, Wednesdays and Saturdays.

This small seventeenth-century farmhouse was the home of Virginia and Leonard Woolf from 1919. They divided their time between Monk's House and their London home, entertaining their friends in the Bloomsbury group. Virginia's sister, Vanessa Bell, lived with Duncan Grant at nearby Charleston Farmhouse.

In 1940, when their London home was bombed, they moved to Rodmell, but in 1941 Virginia drowned herself in the nearby river Ouse. Leonard continued to live in the house until his death in 1969. The house contains much of the furniture, paintings and belongings of the Woolfs.

Moorlands, Friars Gate, Crowborough. Telephone 01892 652474. 2 miles (3 km) north of Crowborough off B2188.
Open: April to October, Wednesdays; also at other times for National Gardens Scheme.

Set in a lovely valley on the edge of Ashdown Forest, these gardens cover over 3

High Beeches Garden.

acres (1.2 hectares) and contain ponds and streams and a riverside walk. There are extensive herbaceous borders, rhododendrons and azaleas and fine specimen trees and shrubs with good autumn colours.

Newtimber Place, Newtimber, Hassocks BN6 9BU. Telephone: 01273 833104.
Open: May to August, Thursdays, by appointment.

This very attractive moated manor house dates from 1680, but there has been a house on the site since pre-Norman times. The main feature is the entrance hall, which was decorated with Etruscan-style frescoes in 1750, based on the collection of Sir William Hamilton now in the British Museum, London. The motif of charioteers and goddesses is repeated in the tapestries and chair coverings.

At the back, the house rises sheer from the moat, which has been incorporated into the design of the informal garden.

Nymans Garden, Handcross, Haywards Heath RH17 6EB. Telephone: 01444 400321.
National Trust.
Open: March to October, Wednesday to Sunday and bank holiday Mondays.

This famous garden was conceived by Ludwig Messel, who started planting in 1885; his son continued the work until 1954, when he bequeathed the garden to the National Trust. There are over 30 acres (12 hectares) of gardens with numerous interesting and rare shrubs and flowers, many of them bred here, but Nymans retains a friendly, intimate air. There are some stunning views over the surrounding countryside from the garden. The house, which was built in 1900 in the style of a Tudor manor, was badly damaged in a fire after the Second World War and has been left as a picturesque ruin.

The Old Clergy House, Alfriston. Telephone: 01323 870001. National Trust.
Open: April to October, daily.

This superb timber-framed hall-house, built about 1360, was the first building purchased by the National Trust. The oak framing is filled with wattle and daub and the roof is

Leonardslee Gardens.

thatched. This is the type of building called a 'Wealden hall-house' but differs slightly from others in that a small separate room with no direct access to the house was provided for the housekeeper of the priest (before the Reformation priests were celibate). The house is in a delightful setting on the village green alongside Alfriston church and has been beautifully restored to its original form by the National Trust.

Parham House and Gardens, Parham, Pulborough RH20 4HS. Telephone: 01903 744888.
Open: Easter to October, Wednesday, Thursday, Sunday and bank holiday Monday afternoons.

Parham House, built in 1577, sits in its huge park facing south to the Downs. It is a typical E-shaped Elizabethan house and was carefully restored in the 1920s. Originally Parham was a grange of Westminster Abbey, and some of the fireplaces are thought to come from the original kitchens. The very fine gardens include a beautiful 4 acre (1.6

hectare) walled garden with herbaceous borders, herb garden and orchard. There is also an eighteenth-century landscaped garden with trees, statuary and lake. In the park is a noted heronry (not accessible to visitors) and there is a good picnic area. In 1990 a brick and turf maze was built on the lawn overlooking the Pleasure Pond.

Pashley Manor Gardens, Ticehurst, near Wadhurst TN5 7HE. Telephone: 01580 200692.
Open: mid April to end of September, Tuesday to Thursday, Saturdays and bank holidays.

This attractive tranquil garden is a mixture of formal rose and shrub beds, a moat and ponds. There are some fine mature trees, which include 450-year-old oaks and specimen conifers planted in the mid nineteenth century when the garden was created. There has been much remodelling in recent years, with the creation of many new beds. The manor of Pashley was owned in the fifteenth and sixteenth centuries by the Boleyn family and it is believed that Anne Boleyn, the future queen, stayed here as a child, but the present house (not open) dates from 1550. A Queen Anne façade and terrace were added to the back in 1720 and overlook the garden.

Petworth House, Petworth GU28 0AE. Telephone: 01798 342207. National Trust.
Open: house, April to October, Tuesday to Thursday, Saturdays and Sundays; park, all year, daily.

Petworth has been the southern home of the Percy family since about 1150. Licence to crenellate was granted to this powerful family in 1309, but only a part of their building remains. Elizabeth, the widow of Sir Harry 'Hotspur' Percy, and the 'gentle Kate' of Shakespeare's *The Taming of the Shrew*, lived for a time in this house and met her second husband, Thomas Camoys, here (see also Trotton church, page 53). In 1682 the Percy heiress married the sixth Duke of Somerset and he, with the help of his wife's inheritance, built the present house. The exterior is mainly remembered for its magnificent west front. Inside, the splendid Painted Staircase, the Marble Hall and the Saloon, with some of Grinling Gibbons's greatest work, are all from the original building of about 1690. In the eighteenth century the house passed by marriage to the Earls of Egremont and the third Earl added the sculpture gallery in 1780. From the seventeenth century successive owners of Petworth have been great collectors of art, and the collection, which includes Van Dycks, Lelys and Turners, is one of the most distinguished in England. Turner was a regular visitor to the house and is well represented in the collection. As splendid as the house is the magnificent park covering over 2000 acres (800 hectares) and laid out by 'Capability' Brown. Deer roam the park and there are many Turner paintings of it.

Priest House, West Hoathly, near East Grinstead RH19 4PP. Telephone: 01342 810479. A Sussex Past property.
Open: April to October, daily.

This very attractive hall-house dates from the early fifteenth century and was built by the Priory of St Pancras at Lewes. Despite its name, it was probably constructed for use as an estate office to administer the property of the priory in and around West Hoathly. About 1600 the owner built a central chimney and divided the house horizontally to provide an upper floor. The house is now used as a museum and is set in a delightful country garden.

Royal Pavilion, Brighton BN1 1EE. Telephone: 01273 603005.
Open: daily, except Christmas Eve and Christmas Day.

This was the marine palace of the Prince Regent, who later became George IV. Following his secret marriage to Mrs Fitzherbert, the Prince rented a farmhouse at Brighton, which Henry Holland converted to a Palladian-style villa in 1786. Some years later the Prince became enamoured with Indian and oriental designs and he appointed the architect John Nash to redesign the Pavilion. The result is the building we know today, a fantastic combination of Indian-style exterior and chinoiserie internal decoration. It took Nash seven years to complete, between 1815 and 1822, but by the time it was finished the king increasingly shunned public life; he last visited the Pavilion in 1827 and died in 1830. An extensive restoration programme, begun in the early 1980s, is now complete and the building can be seen in its full glory. In particular, the Music Room is a spectacular riot of decoration. On the upper floor guest bedrooms, breakfast rooms and Queen Victoria's apartments have been painstakingly recreated. The rooms are arranged with contemporary furniture and works of art, including many pieces on loan from Her Majesty the Queen. The gardens have also been restored to their Regency plan.

Sackville College, High Street, East Grinstead RH19 3AZ. Telephone: 01342 323279 or 326561.
Open: June to August, Wednesday to Saturday.

These almshouses were founded in 1609 by the second Earl of Dorset and completed in 1619. Built of local sandstone and roofed with Horsham slabs, the buildings are attractively grouped around a courtyard. They are

The Royal Pavilion at Brighton was remodelled for the Prince Regent by John Nash, with Indian-style exterior and chinoiserie interior.

still under the patronage of a descendant of the Sackvilles, Earl De La Warr, and are home to eighteen elderly people from the area. The public rooms are open to the public, including the banqueting room with its attractive hammerbeam roof.

St Mary's, Bramber BN44 3WE. Telephone: 01903 816205.
Open: Easter to September, Sunday and Monday afternoons.
St Mary's dates from 1470 and is classified as 'the best late fifteenth-century timber-framing in Sussex'. Fine woodwork includes wall panelling, carved fireplaces and furniture. The unique Painted Room was created for the visit of Queen Elizabeth I. Of special interest are the collection of first editions and illustrated books of Thomas Hood, the nineteenth-century humorous poet and artist, and a superb display of costume dolls. There are charming gardens with amusing topiary.

Sheffield Park Gardens, Uckfield TN22 3QY. Telephone: 01825 790655. National Trust.
Open: March, weekends; April to November, Tuesday to Sunday and bank holiday Mondays.
These magnificent gardens were originally laid out by 'Capability' Brown and Humphry Repton for the first Earl of Sheffield. Nearly 100 acres (40 hectares) of gardens, incorporating a series of lakes, waterfalls and watery vistas, are planted with shrubs and trees, many of them chosen for their autumnal colours by Arthur Soames in the early twentieth century. This is a garden for all seasons, but autumn is particularly spectacular with breathtaking colours on the trees surrounding the lakes. Spring, with its azaleas, rhododendrons and spring flowers is also very beautiful. Sheffield Park House, which can be seen from the gardens, is not owned by the National Trust.

Standen, East Grinstead RH19 4NE. Telephone: 01342 323029. National Trust.
Open: late March, weekends; April to October, Wednesday to Sunday and bank holiday Mondays.
Designed in 1894 by Philip Webb, this is one of his finest houses. The interior is particularly interesting for the William Morris

Standen has a fine interior decorated with William Morris textiles and wallpapers.

textiles and wallpapers, many of them original and others carefully restored from original designs. The original electrical fittings have also been restored. There is an attractive series of terraced gardens looking out over the High Weald and nearby woodland walks.

Stansted House, Rowlands Castle PO9 6DX. Telephone: 01705 412265.
Open: Easter Sunday and Monday; July to September, Sunday to Tuesday and bank holidays.

Originally built in 1686, the house was burnt out in 1900 and rebuilt in neo-Wren style. The elegant rooms contain a good collection of furniture, pictures and porcelain. Set in beautiful countryside, the extensive grounds contain an arboretum and a walled garden. The long avenue was laid out in the eighteenth century and was claimed by Nairn to be one of the best in England, but it was much damaged in the great storm of 1987.

Uppark, South Harting, Petersfield GU31 5QR. Telephone: 01730 825857. National Trust.
Open: June to October, Sunday to Thursday afternoons. Pre-booking is strongly advised – telephone 01730 825317.

This lovely Wren-style house, on the crest of the Downs, was designed and built for the first Lord Tankerville by William Talman in 1690. It was a technological novelty made possible only by the invention of a pump by Lord Tankerville's grandfather which brought water from a spring further down the hill. The approach to the house is so steep that when the house was, at a later date, offered to the Duke of Wellington, he declined it, saying he had 'crossed the Alps once'.

In 1810 Humphry Repton remodelled the house adding two flanking buildings, the stables and kitchens, which were connected by underground passageways, and added a new entrance to the north front. Two notable visitors to the house were Emma Hamilton, later to become Lord Nelson's mistress, and H. G. Wells, whose mother was for some time the housekeeper. Until 1989 the rooms were still decorated with their original eighteenth-

Sheffield Park Gardens.

century wallpapers and fabrics, but in August of that year a fire destroyed much of the interior. The fire started in the roof during the daytime and visitors and staff rescued much of the furniture and pictures but the house was left as a burnt-out shell. The National Trust decided to restore the house to its original condition, reopening it to the public on 1st June 1995. The gardens today are open parkland but it is believed that originally there were formal terraced gardens.

Wakehurst Place, Ardingly, Haywards Heath RH17 6TN. Telephone: 01444 892701. National Trust.
Open: daily, except Christmas Day and New Year's Day.

This 200 acre (80 hectare) garden is noted for its fine collection of rare trees and flowering shrubs. Near the house, which retains part of its sixteenth-century façade, are formal lawns and gardens and from these paths lead down to a series of ponds and lakes. These ponds were originally hammer ponds, and they lie in a heavily wooded valley which, apart from the rare species, displays some of the oaks which are remnants of the old Wealden forests. Along one walk are boulder outcrops of the Sussex sandstone escarpment;

another, the Himalayan Glade, is especially attractive at rhododendron time, but Wakehurst is very much a garden for all seasons. The garden was started by Gerald Loder in 1903 and when it was transferred to the National Trust in 1965 it was leased to the Royal Botanic Garden, Kew, as an outpost. The higher rainfall, undulating slopes and richer soils give a wider range of growing conditions than in London. Parts of the house are now open. There is some fine Jacobean woodwork, and there is a good exhibition on the history of the house and estate.

West Dean Gardens, West Dean, Chichester PO18 0QZ. Telephone: 01243 811303.
Open: April to October, daily.

In a tranquil setting in the South Downs, this 35 acre (14 hectare) garden features specimen trees, herbaceous borders, water gardens, a pergola 300 feet (95 metres) long, a gazebo and a wild garden. The restored walled kitchen garden retains its Edwardian atmosphere; its thirteen splendid historic glasshouses are filled with ferns, sub-temperate and cool house plants. Visitors can enjoy the 2¼ mile (3.6 km) circuit walk through St Roches Arboretum to the crest of the Downs.

8
Museums and galleries

Amberley

Amberley Chalk Pits Museum, Houghton Bridge, Amberley, Arundel BN18 9LT. Telephone: 01798 831370.

Open: April to October, Wednesday to Sunday and bank holidays.

Opened in 1979, the museum aims to show the development of typical industries of south-east England. Situated in 36 acres (15 hectares) of a former chalk quarry, this is a working open-air museum. Exhibits include the limekilns, once the largest works in the area, locomotive sheds, blacksmith's shop, narrow-gauge railway and a brickmaking works. There are also a number of vintage buses and many other exhibits, as well as a nature trail and picnic area.

Arundel

Arundel Museum and Heritage Centre, 61 High Street, Arundel BN18 9AJ. Telephone: 01903 882268.

Open: Easter to October, daily except Sunday mornings.

This museum is devoted to the history of Arundel; the story of the town and its inhabitants is told by means of models, dioramas, pictures, documents and other artefacts. Old photographs of townsfolk and the garments, tools and implements of local craftsmen are displayed in realistic settings.

Arundel Toy and Military Museum, Dolls House, 23 High Street, Arundel BN18 9AD. Telephone: 01903 507446 or 882908.

Open: Easter to October, most days; rest of the year, weekends only, or by arrangement.

Housed in a delightful Georgian cottage, the museum has an extensive and interesting private collection of old toys, games, teddy bears, puppets and dolls, including lead soldiers, tin toys, dolls' houses and rocking horses from the nineteenth century to the

present day. There is also a display of small militaria, curiosities and much more.

Battle

Battle and District Historical Society Museum, Memorial Hall, High Street, Battle TN33 0AQ.

Open: Easter to October, daily, except Sunday mornings.

This small museum has exhibits on the Romano-British remains found locally and from the Sussex iron industry. There is also a nineteenth-century reproduction of the Bayeux Tapestry.

Battle Town Model, The Almonry, High Street, Battle TN33 0EA. Telephone: 01424 772727.

Open: daily, except Sunday.

The Almonry, with its attractive walled garden, dates from the thirteenth century and now houses the town model which gives an overview of the town's history in sound and light.

Buckleys Yesterday's World, 89-90 High Street, Battle TN33 0AQ. Telephone: 01424 775378.

Open: all year, daily.

This popular museum enables the whole family to explore recreated shop and room displays, such as a Victorian kitchen, grocer's and chemist's shops, a 1930s railway station and many more. There are push-button commentaries, smells and a nostalgic video show. Visitors meet an animated and speaking lifesize figure of Queen Victoria in the Royalty Room, where her nightdress and silk stockings are on display. Other attractions include a country garden, an old-fashioned penny arcade, a children's play village, a toddlers' activity area, a miniature golf course, a picnic site and a themed gift shop.

'Bayleaf', the Wealden hall-house at the Weald and Downland Open Air Museum, Singleton.

Lambing time at Farm World, Beckley.

Bexhill

Bexhill Museum, Egerton Road, Bexhill TN39 3HL. Telephone: 01424 211769.
Open: February to December, Tuesday to Sunday.
This well laid-out museum contains collections relating to the natural history, geology and archaeology of Sussex and the history of Bexhill. Although it is primarily a local museum, there are exhibits of a more general character and a programme of temporary exhibitions.

Museum of Costume and Social History, Manor Gardens, Upper Sea Road, Bexhill TN40 1RL. Telephone: 01424 210045.
Open: April to October, daily; and for one week over the New Year period.
Pleasantly situated in the grounds of the Old Manor House, the museum exhibits a wide range of costumes dating from 1760 to 1960. There is also a good collection of fascinating accessories, dolls, toys and other bygones.

Bognor Regis

Bognor Regis Local History Museum, Hotham Park Lodge, High Street, Bognor Regis. Telephone: 01243 823140.
Open: May to September, Wednesday, Friday to Sunday and bank holiday Mondays.
This small local museum displays exhibits relating to the history of Bognor and the surrounding district. The permanent exhibition, which includes a reconstructed nineteenth-century kitchen, is supplemented by various temporary displays and exhibitions.

Brighton

Booth Museum of Natural History, 194 Dyke Road, Brighton BN1 5AA Telephone: 01273 552586.
Open: Monday to Wednesday, Fridays and Saturdays, Sunday afternoons. Closed Good Friday, Christmas Day, Boxing Day and New Year's Day.
Edward Thomas Booth, born in 1840, devoted much of his time to his favourite pastime, collecting birds. The museum was originally built to house his private collection, which he stuffed and cased himself, display-

ing them in natural settings. He bequeathed the museum and collection to Brighton Corporation; several other collections have been added, making this one of the best collections in Britain.
There is a well thought-out gallery illustrating the evolution and adaptation of animal skeletons and an interesting exhibit on the effects of man on the environment.

Brighton Fishing Museum, 201 Kings Road Arches, Brighton BN1 1NB.
Open: July and September, Saturdays, Sundays and weekday afternoons; rest of year, afternoons when the weather is fine.
This small museum was opened in 1994 and has been set up in an arch given to the fishing community in the nineteenth century as a community hall for lectures and social events. The centrepiece of the museum is a traditional Sussex coast fishing boat rigged for sea. There are displays of prints and models, and video and sound tapes tracing the history of the fishing industry.

Brighton Museum and Art Gallery, Church Street, Brighton BN1 1UE Telephone: 01273 603005.
Open: daily, except Wednesdays and Sunday mornings.
The museum and gallery are housed in the stables and riding school originally designed for the Prince Regent. The collection includes old masters, watercolours, fine and applied art, Art Nouveau and Art Deco. There are exhibitions of archaeology, ethnography and furniture and the Willett Collection of pottery and porcelain. There is also a very fine gallery of fashion which illustrates the social uses of clothes and the changes in fashion from 1800 to the present day.

Preston Manor, Preston Road, Brighton BN1 6SD. Telephone: 01273 603005.
Open: Tuesday to Saturday; Sunday and Monday, afternoons only.
This charming Georgian house dates mainly from 1739 and was bequeathed to Brighton Corporation in 1932 by Sir Charles Thomas-Stanford. The interior has been left substantially as it was in his day and contains

a notable collection of English and continental furniture from the seventeenth to nineteenth centuries, silver and ceramics. The Macquoid Bequest, a fine collection of silver, furniture and paintings, is housed in the former library.

Sussex Toy and Model Museum, 52-55 Trafalgar Street, Brighton BN1 4EB. Telephone: 01273 749494.
Open: all year, except Christmas.
This attractive museum housed in the arches under Brighton railway station contains a collection of dolls and teddy bears, planes, forts and trains and has something to interest children of all ages.

Chichester
Chichester District Museum, 29 Little London, Chichester PO19 1PB. Telephone: 01243 784683.
Open: Tuesday to Saturday.
The museum is concerned with the changing lives of people in Chichester and the surrounding area. It is housed in an eighteenth-century former corn store. The galleries are devoted to local history, archaeology and geology. Larger objects are on open display. Interesting exhibits include the mobile city stocks, the municipal 'moon' which lit the way for the mayor, and a half-scale model of a Roman legionary. There are displays on the market town and Chichester since 1900.

Guildhall Museum, Priory Park, Chichester. Telephone: 01243 784683.
Open: June to September, Saturday afternoons only; at other times by appointment.
The fine building which houses this museum was built as a church for Franciscan friars about 1280. Architectural wall painting of the period survives. The building was later used as the town hall and courtroom, where William Blake was tried for sedition. There are interpretative displays on the building and park and larger objects on display include monumental stonework, as well as social history items.

Mechanical Music and Doll Collection, Church Road, Portfield, Chichester PO19

4HN. Telephone: 01243 785421 or 372646.
Open: Easter to September, Sunday to Friday; October to Easter, Sunday only, but closed in December.
This unusual museum, housed in a Victorian church, focuses on several aspects of the late Victorian era. As well as the fascinating collection of mechanical music machines ranging from music boxes to fair organs there are other devices such as early phonographs, bicycles and motorcycles. Equally intriguing are the stereoscopic viewers and magic lantern, and the doll collection is a delight.

Pallant House Gallery, 9 North Pallant, Chichester PO19 1TJ. Telephone: 01243 774557.
Open: Tuesday to Saturday.
Built in 1712 for a prosperous wine merchant, Henry Peckham, Pallant House is one of Chichester's finest Georgian buildings. It is also known as the Dodo House from the comic stone birds on the gateway which are intended to be ostriches, the Peckham crest. The restored building is now open as a furnished house and gallery and contains the Walter Hussey Collection, the gift of a former Dean of Chichester. There is also a fine collection of Bow china.

Ditchling
Ditchling Museum, Church Lane, Ditchling, Hassocks BN6 8TB. Telephone: 01273 844744.
Open: Easter to October, daily; winter, Saturdays and Sundays.
This splendid and unusual museum is housed in the Old School. There are sections devoted to almost every aspect of daily life in England through the ages, illustrated in dioramas, tableaux, models in costume and artefacts. Special exhibitions are held every six weeks.

Eastbourne
Coastal Defence Museum, Wish Tower, King Edward's Parade, Eastbourne. See Tower 73, page 72.

Heritage Centre, 2 Carlisle Road, Eastbourne BN21 4JJ. Telephone: 01323 411189.

Open: April to September, daily.

This small museum houses a permanent exhibition which traces the development of Eastbourne from a small hamlet to the 'Empress of Watering Places'.

'How We Lived Then' Museum of Shops, 20 Cornfield Terrace, Eastbourne BN21 4NS. Telephone: 01323 737143.
Open: daily.

Housed in a late Regency town house, dating from 1850, the museum is a fascinating glimpse of shopping and social life over the last century. One of the oldest collections of its type, it contains well over 75,000 exhibits acquired since about 1960 by Jan and Graham Upton and shown on four floors of authentic old shops, room settings and other displays.

Museum of the Royal National Lifeboat Institution, King Edward's Parade, Eastbourne BN21 4BY. Telephone: 01323 730717.
Open: March to December, daily.

This was the world's first lifeboat museum; opened in 1937, it has a comprehensive collection of lifeboats and equipment. The range starts with oar-propelled boats and continues up to the most modern. There is also a collection of ships in bottles, many photographs and other items. The museum is housed in the former boathouse, which was built in 1897, by public subscription, in memory of the actor William Terriss, who was stabbed to death outside the Adelphi Theatre in London.

Sussex Combined Services Museum, Redoubt Fortress, Royal Parade, Eastbourne. See page 72.

Towner Art Gallery and Local History Museum, Old Town, Eastbourne BN20 8BB. Telephone: 01323 411688.
Open: Wednesday to Sunday.

Housed in an attractive Georgian manor house, which dates from 1776 and is set in pleasant gardens, the collection contains nineteenth- and twentieth-century British paintings, prints and Georgian caricatures. There are also watercolours of Sussex and topographical pictures of old Eastbourne. The museum shows the history and development

of the district from prehistoric times. There is an impressive model of a palaeolithic flint miner at work and a Victorian kitchen.

East Grinstead

Town Museum, East Court, College Lane, East Grinstead RH19 3LT.
Open: Wednesday and Saturday afternoons.

This small museum is devoted to the history of the town and its people. The permanent displays are supplemented from time to time by temporary exhibitions.

Filching

Filching Manor Motor Museum, Filching, near Polegate BN26 5QA. Telephone: 01323 487838.
Open: Easter to May and October, Thursday to Sunday; May to September, daily; November to Easter, weekends only.

This fifteenth-century Wealden hall-house set in 28 acres (11 hectares) of formal gardens is home to some of the rarest racing cars in the world. The collection includes a 1907 Corbin 'Vanderbilt Cup' racer, Alfa Romeos and Bugattis and also Sir Malcolm Campbell's

The Pallant (or Dodo) House, Chichester.

Bluebird speedboat. The hall is of interest in its own right and contains some fine oak panelling, furniture, clocks and antiques. There is also a picnic site.

Halland

Bentley Motor Museum, Halland. See Bentley Wildfowl Reserve, page 110.

Hastings

Fisherman's Museum, Rock-a-Nore, Hastings TN34 3DW. Telephone: 01424 424787.
Open: Easter to September, daily except Saturday.

This museum is in the former fishermen's church, on the beach amongst the old net shops; it contains many interesting items relating to local fishing. The chief exhibit is the lugger *Enterprise*, built at Rock-a-Nore in 1909 and shown rigged for sea. There are a number of models and the last horse capstans which were used for hauling the boats up the beach. Of more recent interest is the painting of Sir Winston Churchill receiving his golden winkle when being made a member of the Winkle Club in 1955. The museum takes a special interest in the restoration and upkeep of the nearby net shops, which are believed to date from Tudor times.

Hastings Museum and Art Gallery, John's Place, Cambridge Road, Hastings TN34 1ET. Telephone: 01424 781100.
Open: daily.

The varied collection in this museum includes special features on dinosaurs and local wildlife as well as displays of ceramics, fine art and examples of the local ironworking industry. Attached to the museum is the Durbar Hall, a reconstruction of an Indian palace built in 1886 and containing a collection of oriental art and Pacific ethnology. Two new galleries on North American Indians opened in the spring of 1995.

Museum of Local History, Old Town Hall, High Street, Hastings TN34 3EW. Telephone: 01424 781200.
Open: October to December and March, every afternoon except Wednesday; Easter to September, Tuesday to Sunday.

Once the town hall, this building now houses a small attractive museum. The ground floor contains a chronological display of exhibits relating to the history of the town, including a model of the battle of Hastings. The upstairs galleries illustrate many facets of local life: industries, pastimes, smuggling and maritime history.

Shipwreck Heritage Centre, Rock-a-Nore Road, Hastings TN34 3DW. Telephone: 01424 437452.
Open: April to September, daily.

The centre focuses on a series of seventeenth- to twentieth-century wrecks which are visible nearby at low tides. Photographs, videos and artefacts from the wrecks, including an American Civil War gun-runner, provide a fascinating exhibition. A 'sound and light' show traces the story of a ship which sank in the Thames through five centuries of maritime history to its discovery and rescue in 1970. Radar and video equipment which monitor the traffic in the English Channel are also on display.

Horsham

Horsham Museum, Causeway House, 9 The Causeway, Horsham RH12 1HE. Telephone: 01403 454959.
Open: Tuesday to Saturday.

The museum is housed in an attractive sixteenth-century half-timbered building in a pleasant part of Horsham. The museum has displays on ceramics, furniture, social life, exotica, costume, local history and punishment. There are reconstructed wheelwright's and blacksmith's shops and a saddler's shop featuring the Albery Collection of saddlery and bits. At the rear of the museum around the Centenary Garden are a gallery on farming life and a gallery on transport featuring the museum's collection of early bicycles. There is a small permanent display on the poet Shelley, including many first and early editions. The museum also houses the Albery Collection of manuscripts on the history of the town.

Hove

British Engineerium, Neville Road, Hove BN3 7QA. Telephone: 01273 559583.

This unusual bicycle is among the exhibits at Horsham Museum.

Open: daily; steam up on Sundays and bank holidays.

This fascinating museum offers a glimpse of the technology and craftsmanship of the Victorian age and is based in the Goldstone Pumping Station, which commenced operation in 1866 and supplied, as it still does, much of the water for Brighton and Hove. Water was raised 160 feet (50 metres) by means of steam-operated pumps but soon after the Second World War electric pumps were installed in the wells and the steam pumps left to decay. In 1971, when it was proposed to pull down the station and scrap the equipment, the efforts of enthusiasts enabled a preservation order to be placed on the building and restoration work to start. In 1976 the Number 2 beam engine was restarted, almost exactly one hundred years after its installation, and the museum opened to the public. Apart from the great beam engines, there are railway engines, fire engines, steam rollers and numerous full-size and model engines, as well as machines and hand tools which relate to the development of steam power. Numerous special exhibitions are held and the museum runs a number of practical courses in the history of engineering.

Hove Museum and Art Gallery, 19 New Church Road, Hove BN3 4AB. Telephone: 01273 779410.
Open: Tuesday to Sunday.

The museum contains a good collection of English paintings, miniatures, pottery, glass and silver from the seventeenth century to the twentieth. A special gallery is devoted to Hove's pioneer film-makers, with a permanent video showing the town in 1900. For younger visitors, the Childhood Gallery looks at every aspect of children's life in a room crammed with toys and interactive exhibits.

Lewes

Anne of Cleves House Museum, 52 Southover High Street, Lewes BN7 1JA. Telephone: 01273 474610. A Sussex Past property.
Open: April to October, Monday to Saturday, and Sunday afternoons; November, January to March, Tuesday to Thursday, and by appointment.

The museum is housed in a lovely timber-framed building which dates from the sixteenth century and was given to Anne of Cleves as part of her divorce settlement from Henry VIII. The rooms have been arranged to show the construction of the building and to give an impression of life in the house during the seventeenth and eighteenth centuries. The restful garden is laid out in Tudor style. The galleries contain an interesting collection of toys, games and domestic items of mainly local interest. There is also a very well-illustrated display of ironwork from the Sussex iron industries.

Museum of Sussex Archaeology, Barbican House, 169 High Street, Lewes BN7 1YE. Telephone: 01273 486290. A Sussex Past property.
Open: daily.

This excellent little museum charts man's progress in Sussex from earliest to medieval times. Well laid-out galleries are used to display models and artefacts which emphasise the way of life. The museum is housed in an Elizabethan building by the Barbican Gate of Lewes Castle and is run by the Sussex Archaeological Society. Also contained within the museum is the Lewes Living History Model, a town model recreating the town as it was a century ago and which uses an audio-visual display to highlight the town's long history.

Littlehampton

Littlehampton Museum, Manor House, Church Street, Littlehampton BN17 5EP. Telephone: 01903 715149.
Open: Tuesday to Saturday.

This small museum has displays relating to the local history, archaeology, art and maritime history of Littlehampton and district. It has an active programme of temporary exhibitions, covering a wide variety of different themes.

Newhaven

Newhaven Local and Maritime History Museum, West Foreshore, Newhaven. Telephone: 01273 514760.
Open: Easter to October, Saturdays, Sundays and bank holidays.

This small museum was founded by the Newhaven Historical Society and is run and maintained by its members. It has a good collection of exhibits of local and maritime interest and an excellent collection of photographic records of the town and port.

Robertsbridge

Museum of Rural Life, Northbridge Street, Robertsbridge TN32 5NY. Telephone: 01580 880324.
Open: daily.

There is a varied collection of exhibits in this small museum which is adjacent to a working blacksmith's forge. There are reconstructed interiors of wheelwright's, grocery, hardware and other shops, and a collection of country implements and a garage workshop. A large collection of iron firebacks is a reminder of the local iron industry.

Rottingdean

Rottingdean Grange, The Green, Rottingdean, Brighton BN2 7HA. Telephone: 01273 301004.
Open: daily.

This early Georgian house was originally the vicarage and was given its present name, The Grange, by the artist Sir William Nicolson, who lived here before the First World War. The building was altered and enlarged by Sir Edwin Lutyens in the 1920s and now contains a library on the ground floor and a gallery and museum above. The museum and gallery were closed in 1992 by Brighton Corporation but in 1994 they were leased to Rottingdean Preservation Society, which has reopened them. The exhibits include a reconstruction of Rudyard Kipling's study, complete with a life-sized model of the author, along with memorabilia. Kipling lived for some years in Rottingdean in The Elms, just across The Green from the museum. There is also a permanent display based on Bob Copper, another village resident, who together with his family has done much to preserve the tradition of Sussex folksongs, and whose recollections of life in Rottingdean between the two World Wars recall the rural days of the village.

The Museum of Rural Life at Robertsbridge.

Rye

Rye Heritage Centre, The Old Sail Loft, Strand Quay, Rye TN31 7AY. Telephone: 01797 226696.
Open: April to October, daily; winter, Saturdays and Sundays.

The centre houses the Rye Town Model, a splendid model of the town which uses sound and light to trace the history of the ancient borough. The life and atmosphere of the town are dramatically brought to life and the visitor is transported back in time to the fourteenth-century French raids and to the more recent past, with excisemen pursuing smugglers.

Rye Museum, Rye Castle, Gun Garden, Rye TN31 7HH. Telephone: 01797 226728.
Open: Easter to October, daily; winter, weekends.

Housed in the thirteenth-century Ypres Tower, the museum tells the history of Rye and Romney Marsh and has wonderful views over the marsh to the sea.

Seaford

Martello Tower 74, The Esplanade, Seaford. See page 72.

Shoreham-by-Sea

Marlipins Museum, High Street, Shoreham-by-Sea BN43 6TH. Telephone: 01273 462994. A Sussex Past property.
Open: May to September, daily except Monday.

The museum is housed in one of the oldest secular buildings in England, dating from the twelfth century; it was originally the custom house, for collecting ships' tolls. The building was refaced in the fourteenth century with its present striking chequerwork of flint and Caen stone. It is a small but expanding museum, with emphasis on the ancient port of Shoreham, and has one of the best collections of old Sussex maps in the county. There is a fine display of paintings of maritime scenes and of nautical models.

Singleton

Weald and Downland Open Air Museum, Singleton, Chichester PO18 0EU. Telephone: 01243 811348. 5 miles (8 km) north of Chichester on A286.
Open: March to October, daily; November to February, Sundays and Wednesdays.

This is a delightful museum, in both concept and position. Situated on a 45 acre (18 hectare) site in the lovely Lavant valley, the museum contains a continually expanding collection of historic buildings which have been saved from destruction and re-erected on the site. The museum opened to the public in 1971; there are nearly forty buildings including a medieval farmstead with its house, furniture and farm livestock, a working watermill, a village school, rural craft workshops and a Tudor market hall. A 'hands on' gallery explores building materials and techniques. Visitors may picnic by the millpond or walk in attractive woods where charcoal is made. Longport House, a farmhouse from the Channel Tunnel site, forms a new reception centre, opened in 1995.

Steyning

Steyning Museum, Church Street, Steyning BN44 3YB. Telephone: 01903 813333.
Open: Tuesdays, Wednesdays, Fridays, Saturdays and Sundays.

This local museum traces Steyning's history from a Saxon port to a successful market town with fine Tudor buildings. Displays include Roman pottery, tableaux of its station and 400-year-old school, and objects of agricultural and domestic life.

Tangmere

Tangmere Military Aviation Museum, Tangmere Airfield, Tangmere, Chichester PO20 6ES. Telephone: 01243 775223.
Open: February to November, daily.

One of the most famous Battle of Britain airfields, Tangmere now houses a collection of planes and other artefacts which give a fascinating glimpse of the airfield's history and of aerial warfare over Sussex. It covers seventy years of aviation history. Maps, documents, photographs and uniforms are amongst the smaller exhibits, whilst the larger ones include Hunter, Meteor and Swift jet fighters. There are full-size replicas of the Spitfire and Hurricane, as well as displays and working exhibits.

Winchelsea

Court Hall Museum, Court Hall, High Street, Winchelsea TN36 4EA. Telephone: 01797 224395.
Open: Easter to mid May, Saturday and Sunday; mid May to September, Tuesday to Sunday.

The Court Hall is the oldest building in Winchelsea and now houses an interesting collection of exhibits mainly relating to the town's period as a member of the Cinque Ports Confederation. There is also a town model and displays showing the effects of coastline changes which left the town cut off from the sea.

Worthing

Worthing Museum and Art Gallery, Chapel Road, Worthing BN11 1HP. Telephone: 01903 239999.
Open: Monday to Saturday.

The museum contains displays of archaeology, geology and the history of Worthing and its surroundings. A major exhibit is the Saxon grave finds from the excavations on nearby Highdown Hill; these include glass and jewellery. There is a large collection of costumes and a special children's corner with displays of dolls, toys and games. The gallery contains a good collection of oil paintings and watercolours by British artists of the eighteenth to twentieth centuries. The museum has a sculpture garden and there is a varied programme of temporary exhibitions.

9
Industrial heritage

The economy of Sussex today is largely based on agriculture and service industries and has little of what might be termed heavy industry. The impression gained is one of an essentially rural and residential countryside and it is difficult to imagine that this was once a major iron-producing area and the industrial heartland of England. Little remains of the structures of the industry today except the 'hammer ponds', many of which have been converted to ornamental ponds and lakes. A number of churches, including Burwash, Rotherfield, Salehurst, Sedlescombe, Wadhurst and West Hoathly, have iron gravestones and tomb slabs and at Ninfield there are iron stocks and a whipping post on the village green.

A small gunpowder industry existed in the nineteenth century in the east of the county, but little remains except the names of fields and lanes, for example Powdermill Lane in Battle.

Before the age of steam, mechanical power was provided by waterwheels and windmills, used mainly for grinding corn, for raising water and draining marshes and to operate sawmills and, in some cases, farm machinery. The earliest windmills were the post mills, named from the large post on which the mills were turned to face the wind. Later, it was realised that only the sweeps needed to be turned and the smock mill and the tower mill were devised.

With the arrival of steam power, windmills and watermills declined in importance and many were allowed to decay and fall down. However, many owners, local authorities and preservation societies have made great efforts to save some and the county is fortunate in having a number of restored mills. The arrival of steam power also brought the railways and within twenty-five years from the first in 1839 all the main lines into Sussex were completed. The railways expanded and developed an industry which is still very important to the Sussex economy – tourism.

Another visible symbol of the industrial heritage is the oasthouse, a distinctive landmark particularly in the east of the county. Most date from the early years of the nineteenth century, when the hopping industry expanded rapidly, providing employment not only for local people but for many casual workers from London up to the 1940s. Mechanisation and new methods of drying hops diminished the labour requirements of the industry and many oasthouses became redundant. Some were allowed to decay and others were converted to private dwellings although strict local planning regulations have retained their distinctive silhouette in the landscape.

The following list gives a selection of accessible sites which are representative of the industrial past. In addition to these sites, there are a number of other well-restored windmills which are on private land and not open to the public, although they are distinctive landmarks.

Ashburnham iron furnace (OS 199: TQ 685170). On a track leading north from the Penhurst to Ponts Green road.

Not much remains of this, the last working iron furnace in Sussex, other than the brick wheel-pit, but it is worth a visit to stand in this quiet rural area and try to imagine it going at full blast.

Bartley Mill, Bell's Yew Green, near Frant. Just off the B2169. Telephone: 01892 890372. *Open: daily.*

This watermill was part of a once thriving hop farm and is now milling flour for the first time since the early twentieth century. There is a small museum and a farm trail and picnic area.

Bateman's Watermill, Burwash. Part of the National Trust property at Bateman's (see page 83). Telephone: 01435 882302.

This small mill, restored by volunteers from the Sussex Industrial Archaeology Society, is fully operational and grinds corn for flour. Attached to the wheel is one of the earliest water-driven turbines installed by Rudyard Kipling to provide electricity for the house. In his autobiographical *Something of Myself*, Kipling describes, amusingly, how he was helped in this project by Sir William Willcocks, who had just returned from Egypt where he had built the first Aswan Dam on the river Nile!

Bluebell Railway, Sheffield Park Station, near Uckfield TN22 3QL. Telephone: 01825 722370 (talking timetable), 01825 723777 (general enquiries). Off A275 between Lewes and East Grinstead.
Open: all year, Saturdays and Sundays; May to September, daily.

The first of the preserved standard-gauge steam railways in Britain, the Bluebell Railway began operation in 1960. There are some 10 miles (16 km) of track, from Sheffield Park to Kingscote, with vintage bus connections to East Grinstead. The authentic period station and unspoilt scenery are often used for film locations.

Burton Mill (OS 197: SU 978180). 2 miles (3 km) south of Petworth, east of A285.
Open: mill, Monday to Wednesday; nature trail, daily.

This eighteenth-century watermill has been restored to full working order and is now driven by a water turbine producing stone-ground flour and cereals. There is a nature trail around the millpond and through the surrounding oak and birch woodlands.

Chailey Windmill, Chailey, near Lewes.
Open: Sundays and bank holidays.

This smock mill is said to be at the exact centre of Sussex. Seven mills have been recorded on the site, the earliest in 1595, but the present one was built at West Hoathly in 1830 and moved to Chailey in 1864. It ceased working in 1911 and has remained idle ever since. A new cap and sweeps were fitted in 1933–5 and the mill was extensively restored again in 1954. It now houses a small museum of rural life.

Clayton Windmills, Clayton, Hassocks. Telephone: 01273 843263.
Open ('Jill' only): May to September, Sundays and bank holidays.

These two mills, called 'Jack' and 'Jill', are one of the best-known landmarks in Sussex. 'Jill', a white-painted post mill, was originally built at Patcham, near Brighton, in 1821 but at some date before 1866 she was hauled over the Downs by a team of oxen to her present site. For some time she worked together with an older post mill built on the site in 1765. In 1866 'Jack', a tile-covered tower mill, was built to replace the earlier mill. The pair now stand high on the Downs above Clayton on the line of the South Downs Way. In 1973 a film company restored 'Jack' for use in a film sequence and it is now a private residence; 'Jill' has been restored by the local authority and is open to the public.

Coultershaw Water Pump. 2 miles (3 km) south of Petworth on A285.
Open: April to September, first and third Sunday of each month.

This water-driven beam pump was originally built in 1784 to pump water from the river Rother to Petworth 1½ miles (2.4 km) away and 150 feet (46 metres) higher up. It has been restored to working order by the Sussex Industrial Archaeology Society and a barn, formerly from Goodwood, has been erected over it to provide a display centre.

East and West Cliff Railways, Hastings. Telephone: 01424 718888.
Open: April to October, daily.

Two cliff railways ascend the east and west cliffs either side of the Old Town at Hastings. The East Cliff railway is the steepest in Britain, having a gradient of 1:1.28. It rises nearly 300 feet (90 metres) to the start of Hastings Country Park, giving spectacular views over the fishing beach and Old Town. Before its electrification in 1974, it was one of the last water-balance railways left in England. The West Cliff railway was built in 1890 and is unique in running for its whole length in a tunnel formed by extending a natural cave in the rock. Nearly 500 feet (154 metres) long, it has a gradient of 1:1.3 and rises to the castle.

Halnaker Windmill (pronounced Hanneker), Halnaker, near Chichester.
Open: at all times.
  One of the oldest surviving mills in Sussex, this tile-covered tower mill was built in 1750 and stands at the top of the Downs, which at this point are over 400 feet (121 metres) high. It ceased working about 1900 and some time after this the interior was filled with chalk to maintain the structure as a landmark for mariners. In 1934 the mill was restored as a memorial to Lady Bird, the wife of Sir William Bird, a watercolour by Turner being used as a reference. During the Second World War the mill was used as an observation tower and in 1955 it was restored again by West Sussex County Council.

High Salvington Windmill, near Worthing.
Open: April to September, first and third Sunday of each month.
  This black weatherboarded post mill is situated some 320 feet (97 metres) up on the Downs with commanding views of Worthing

and the sea. It was built about 1700 and continued working until 1897. In 1912 the old timber roundhouse was converted to a tea room, which continued into the 1950s. There followed a period of neglect but in 1976 a preservation society was formed and the mill is almost completely restored.

Ifield Watermill, Hyde Drive, Ifield, Crawley. Telephone: 01293 523481.
Open: Sundays.
  This four-storey brick and timber mill dates from 1810 but stands on a site occupied by a mill since the seventeenth century. The mill is currently being restored but the waterwheel is working and there are displays of local history.

Kent & East Sussex Railway, Tenterden Town Station, Tenterden, Kent TN30 6HE. Telephone: 01580 223329.
Open: March to December; daily in peak season, weekends only in low season.
  Britain's first light railway, this was constructed in 1900 from Tenterden in Kent to Robertsbridge in East Sussex along the attractive Rother valley. Steam trains now run from Tenterden to Northiam.

The Kent & East Sussex Railway at Northiam.

King's Mill, Shipley, was owned by Hilaire Belloc, the author.

King's Mill, Shipley. 1 mile (1.6 km) south of A272.
Open: May to September, first weekend of each month.

Known locally as Belloc's Mill, after Hilaire Belloc, a former resident of Shipley, this superb white smock mill, the largest working in Sussex, was built in 1879 and is perhaps the finest in the county. It was bought by Belloc in 1906 and ceased working in 1926. From then until the Second World War he tried to keep it in repair but, with labour and materials scarce, it deteriorated. After his death an appeal was launched to restore the mill as a memorial to the author; the work was completed in 1958.

The Lavender Line, Isfield Station, Isfield, near Uckfield TN22 5XB. Telephone: 01825 750515. Off A26.
Open: all year, Saturdays, Sundays and bank holidays; August, daily.

Left derelict in 1969, this attractive Victorian station has been beautifully restored to its former elegance. Unlimited rides are available in the railway's growing collection of locomotives and rolling stock.

Mannings Heath hammer ponds (OS 198: TQ 220290).

On the minor road between Ashfold Crossway and Doomsday Green, two very fine hammer ponds are visible from the road.

Michelham Priory Watermill, Upper Dicker, near Hailsham. Part of Michelham Priory (see page 74). Telephone: 01323 844224. A Sussex Past property.

This working watermill dates from the sixteenth century and is supplied with water from the moat, which is fed from the river Cuckmere. There are also reconstructed wheelwright's and blacksmith's shops on the main site.

Ninfield village green (OS 199: TQ 707124).

On the village green are cast-iron stocks and a whipping post probably made at the Ashburnham forge.

Nutley Windmill, Nutley, near Uckfield.
Open: Easter to September, last Sunday of each month and bank holiday Mondays.

This post mill, the oldest working mill in Sussex, is the smallest of its type in the county and the only example with an open trestle. It was brought from Crowborough about 1813 and ceased operation in 1908. In 1968 the Uckfield and District Preservation Society undertook the task of restoring the mill to working order. The sails turned again in 1972 and the mill became fully operative in 1981.

It stands in a magnificent position overlooking Ashdown Forest.

Polegate Windmill, Polegate. 4 miles (6 km) north of Eastbourne on A22.
Open: Easter to September, Sundays and bank holidays.
This tower mill, complete with sweeps, dates from 1817 and was in use until 1965. The tower is 45 feet (13 metres) high and contains the original applewood machinery. The mill was worked by wind until 1943, when an electric motor was installed. It was repaired and restored after an appeal and there is a small museum adjoining.

Shipley hammer pond (OS 198: TQ 157211).
On a footpath half a mile (800 metres) west of the A24 is one of the largest hammer ponds in the county. The pond served Knepp Furnace near Knepp Castle which was worked from 1568 to 1604.

Volk's Electric Railway, 285 Madeira Drive, Brighton BN2 1EN. Telephone: 01273 681086.
Open: March to September, daily.
Running between the Palace Pier and Brighton Marina, this was the first electric railway in Britain. Opened in 1883, the railway was built by Magnus Volk, a pioneer in the use of electricity, and the trains carry the insignia VR (Volk's Railway). An extension was built in 1896 to Rottingdean but since it was covered by high tides it was soon abandoned as impracticable.

West Blatchington Windmill, Holmes Avenue, Hove.
Open: May to September, Sundays and bank holidays.
Once part of a small village on the Downs, this unusual hexagonal smock mill is now almost totally surrounded by houses. It dates from the mid eighteenth century and last worked about 1900. The wooden structure sits on top of a flint tower and barns. It has been restored and the sweeps remounted. There is a small museum of milling and farming housed in the buildings.

10
Other places to visit

Arundel Wildfowl and Wetlands Centre, Mill Road, Arundel BN18 9PB. Telephone: 01903 883355.
Open: daily.

There are over 55 acres (22 hectares) of landscaped pens and lakes in this refuge, which is attractively situated between Swanbourne Lake and the river Arun. The refuge is backed by a steep wooded hanger and the battlements of Arundel Castle, and in front are marshes and estuary. Wild ducks, geese and swans can be watched from the hides, which look out over water-meadows, ponds and shallow scrapes for wading species, while the tame wildfowl can be seen on lakes and paths around the reserve. The attractive visitor centre overlooks Swan Lake, the largest in the refuge, and contains an interpretative area with displays and exhibitions and a lovely viewing gallery. A level path connects the hides and ponds, making the refuge suitable for the disabled to visit.

Bentley Wildfowl Reserve, Halland. Telephone: 01825 840573. 7 miles (11 km) northeast of Lewes on B2192.
Open: March to October, daily; also winter weekends.

The reserve was started in 1960 by Gerald Askew as a private collection and opened to the public in 1966. About 25 acres (10 hectares) of land are devoted to the reserve and ponds and lakes have been dug for the birds. There are now over one thousand birds, representing one hundred species; these include geese, ducks, flamingoes and peacocks. The main rooms of Bentley House, a converted Tudor farmhouse, are also open to the public and an additional attraction is the **Motor Museum,** with a good collection of veteran and vintage cars. There is also a woodland walk, a children's small animal section and adventure playground and an excellent picnic area.

Boat trips
Beachy Head
Trips to the lighthouse and cliffs are available daily in season from the beach at Eastbourne.

Bewl Water. Telephone: 01892 890661.
Trips on the lake aboard SS *Frances Mary* are an excellent way to enjoy the beauty of the scenery in this part of the High Weald.

Bodiam Ferry Company. Telephone: 01797 280363.
Trips are run along the river Rother from Newenden, near the Kent & East Sussex Railway terminus at Northiam (page 107), to Bodiam Castle (page 68), with a chance to break the journey at either end.

Chichester Harbour. Telephone: 01243 286418.
Starting from Itchenor, the 1½ hour trip is an ideal way to see this Area of Outstanding Natural Beauty with its seabirds and boats.

River Arun Cruises. Telephone: 01243 265792.
There are cruises from Littlehampton or Arundel along the picturesque Arun river with stopovers at Arundel and Amberley.

Brighton Sea Life Centre, Marine Parade, Brighton BN2 1TB. Telephone: 01273 604234.
Open: daily.

Visitors can discover a remarkable underwater world filled with hundreds of fascinating marine creatures. In one of the largest underwater tunnels in Europe, they come face to face with stingrays, conger eels and British sharks. There are daily talks and displays.

Butlin's Southcoast World, Bognor Regis PO21 1JT. Telephone: 01243 822445.
Open: Easter to October, daily; November to

April, most weekends.

This first-rate family attraction was commended in the England for Excellence Awards in 1991. A single fixed-rate entrance fee gives all-day access to the Aquasplash water fun area, the giant indoor adventure playground, dodgems and other funfair rides and much more. There is also a cafeteria and restaurant.

Butterfly Centre, Royal Parade, Eastbourne BN22 7AQ. Telephone: 01323 645552.
Open: April to October, daily.

The Centre is a large indoor tropical garden, complete with a lake and waterfalls. The lush vegetation includes strelitzia, bougainvillea, hibiscus, passionflower, oleander and lantana and is the natural habitat for the hundreds of exotic butterflies and moths from all parts of the world. The butterflies are flying about as visitors stroll around. They can be studied at close quarters and the eggs, caterpillars and chrysalids observed. Most of the garden is on the level and therefore accessible to the disabled. It is a colourful spectacle ideal for photographers and suitable for all ages.

Coombes Farm Tours, Church Farm, Coombes, Lancing BN15 0RS. Telephone: 01273 452028.
Open: March to October, all trips by prior arrangement.

Here is a chance to see life on a working farm set in over 1000 acres (420 hectares) of beautiful downland scenery, much of it designated an Environmentally Sensitive Area, and rich in wildlife and wildflowers. The tour takes over an hour and a half, riding on a tractor and trailer, visiting all parts of the farm. In the spring lambing can be seen. There is an audiovisual exhibition and facilities for disabled visitors; wheelchairs can go on the trailers by prior arrangement.

Drusillas Park, Alfriston, Polegate BN26 5QS. Telephone: 01323 870234. Off A27 between Lewes and Eastbourne.
Open: daily.

Started over seventy years ago, this small zoo set in the Cuckmere valley at the foot of

the South Downs is considered to be the best in the south of England. The zoo has a wide variety of animals living in cleverly designed natural environments. Learning-related play activities are scattered throughout the zoo to keep even the youngest visitor amused. 'Down on the Farm' has a life-sized cow that children can milk. Other popular habitats include Meerkat Mound, Monkey Mountain, Penguin Bay, Otter Valley, Flamingo Lagoon, Parrot Falls and World of Owls. A railway runs through the paddocks and there is an outdoor play area of 1 acre (0.4 hectare) for children, with a large play barn for rainy days. There are special facilities for the disabled, including the visually impaired.

Earnley Butterflies and Gardens, 113 Aldington Lane, Earnley, near Chichester PO20 7JR. Telephone: 01243 512637.
Open: March to November, daily.

The gardens were started in 1985 as a series of covered gardens based on themes from around the world. To these have been added new gardens where visitors can walk amongst free-flying tropical butterflies and exotic birds. There is also a pets' corner as well as children's play areas.

Farm World, Great Knelle Farm, Beckley, Rye TN31 6UB. Telephone: 01797 260250.
Open: February, weekends only; March to September, daily.

This traditional Sussex farm of over 600 acres (240 hectares) enables visitors to get a good impression of life 'down on the farm'. A tractor train takes visitors around the fields and there is the Children's Farm for young visitors, a picnic site and a go-kart grass track.

Flimwell Bird Park, Hawkhurst Road, Flimwell TN5 7QP. Telephone: 01580 879202.
Open: April to September, daily.

Set in over 14 acres (6 hectares), with lovely views over the surrounding Weald, the park is home to a superb collection of birds: swans, peacocks, ornamental waterfowl, and twenty-four aviaries. There is also a children's playground and a picnic area.

Garden Paradise and Planet Earth, Avis Road, Newhaven. Telephone: 01273 512123.
Open: daily.

There are over 2 acres (0.8 hectare) of landscaped gardens with lakes, waterfalls and a miniature railway and two temperature-controlled plant houses which contrast the fauna of deserts and tropical rain forests. Planet Earth uses a series of tableaux, including motorised dinosaur models, to depict the history of the Earth from its earliest days and to trace the course of civilisation. There is also a garden centre, restaurant and picnic area.

Hastings Embroidery, Town Hall, Hastings. Telephone: 01424 718888.
Open: Monday to Friday.

The Hastings Embroidery is 243 feet (75 metres) long and illustrates English history from 1066 to the present in hand embroidery, appliqué and tapestry. It was woven by the Royal School of Needlework in 1966.

Hastings Sea Life Centre, Rock-a-Nore Road, Hastings TN34 3DW. Telephone: 01424 718776.
Open: daily.

Apart from the tanks containing hundreds of native sea animals, there are touch pools enabling close encounters with crabs and other rock-pool dwellers. The spectacular see-through tunnel enables visitors to 'walk under water' and there is a three-dimensional film show which journeys from outer space to ocean depths.

Holly Gate Cactus Nursery and Garden, Billingshurst Road, Ashington, Pulborough RH20 3BA. Telephone: 01903 892930. Half a mile (800 metres) north of Ashington on B2133.
Open: daily.

A collection of more than twenty thousand plants from the arid areas of North and South America and Africa is housed in over 10,000 square feet (929 square metres) of glass-houses, where visitors can enjoy the landscaped gardens whatever the weather. There are always plants in flower and plenty of them on sale.

Quarry Farm Rural Experience, Bodiam TN32 5XD. Half a mile (800 metres) south of Bodiam. Telephone: 01580 830670.
Open: April to September, Saturdays, Sundays and bank holidays; also daily during school holidays.

Quarry Farm was once part of the extensive Guinness hop farms in this area. It now houses an interesting collection of animals, rural exhibits and steam engines. There is also an adventure playground for children and a farm trail.

Regency Town House Tour, Hove. Telephone: 01273 206306.
By arrangement.

Much of the seafront development of Brighton and Hove between 1820 and 1850, with its fine Regency terraces and crescents, was the architectural creation of Charles Busby and the father and son team of Amon Wilds. This tour concentrates on the Brunswick Estate development in Hove, which was largely the work of Busby, and provides an opportunity to look at his drawings for the project and to visit a 'Regency' town house which is being restored for public exhibition.

Seven Sisters Sheep Centre, Birling Manor Farm, East Dean, near Eastbourne BN20 0DG. Telephone: 01323 423302. 3 miles (5 km) west of Eastbourne off A259.
Open: March to September, daily.

Here you can see sheep-farming at close hand and, depending on the season, watch lambing, shearing, milking and cheesemaking. Over forty different British breeds of sheep are on display along with other young farm animals and in a seventeenth-century flint barn there is an interesting exhibition on the history of the downland sheep.

Smuggler's Adventure, St Clement's Caves, West Hill, Hastings TN34 3HY. Telephone: 01424 422964.
Open: daily.

Over fifty life-sized figures together with models and pictures are used to tell the story of smuggling around the coast of southern England in the eighteenth and nineteenth centuries. The exhibition is housed in St Clement's Caves, which cover over 1 acre (0.4 hectare) and are a partly natural formation, enlarged by sand excavations. There is a museum and an audio-visual show.

Thomas Smith's Trug Shop, Hailsham Road, Herstmonceux BN27 4LH. Telephone: 01232 832137 or 833801.
Open: shop, Monday to Saturday; workshop, Monday to Friday.

Herstmonceux is famous for its trugs, wooden baskets used by gardeners and as items for home decoration. After selling some to Queen Victoria at the Great Exhibition, Thomas Smith, the inventor of the trug, is said to have walked to London in 1851 to deliver his trugs in person to Buckingham Palace. In the workshop visitors can see the craftsmen at work on these traditional Sussex baskets and buy them from the trug shop.

Washbrooks Farm Centre, Hurstpierpoint. Telephone: 01273 832201.
Open: daily.

Here is a chance to see life on a working farm and get close to the animals, including horses, sheep and pigs, as well as ducks and chickens. Tractor rides are usually available and there is a farm trail, children's play area and tearooms.

Wine cellars and vineyards
Vines have been grown in Britain since Roman times but after the Norman Conquest there was easy access to high-quality wines from northern France and so there was less call for the more variable quality of local produce. However, since the 1960s techniques have been developed which enable good wine to be produced even in cold wet seasons. There are now nearly twenty vineyards which are open regularly in Sussex, each with its particular attractions and each offering an opportunity to buy directly.

Arundel Vineyards, The Vineyard, Church Lane, Lyminster, near Arundel. Telephone: 01903 883393.
Open: April to October, Tuesday to Thursday, Saturdays, Sundays and bank holiday Mondays.

The wine can be tasted in a fifteenth-century Sussex barn at this vineyard and winery. There is a vineyard trail, a collection of old agricultural implements and a picnic area.

Barkham Manor Vineyard, Piltdown, Uckfield TN22 3XE. Telephone: 01825 722103.
Open: April to December, daily.

There are guided tours and a vineyard trail around the vines and winery on this historic site. Barkham Manor was mentioned in Domesday, although the present house dates only from the 1830s, and Piltdown was the site of the 'discovery' of the notorious Piltdown Man. There is a shop adjoining a lovely eighteenth-century thatched barn and a picnic area.

Barnsgate Manor Vineyard, Heron's Ghyll, near Uckfield. Telephone: 01825 713366.
Open: daily.

This vineyard is part of a larger Wealden farm with excellent views to the Downs. Apart from the usual attractions of a trail and tasting, there is a small museum, tearooms and a restaurant. Unusually, there is also a herd of llamas.

Bookers Vineyard, Foxhole Lane, Bolney, near Haywards Heath. Telephone: 01444 881575.
Open: daily except Mondays.

There are 5 acres (2 hectares) of vines with a trail; guided tours are available by arrangement.

Breaky Bottom Vineyard, Rodmell, Lewes BN7 3EX. Telephone: 01273 476427.
Open: daily.

Beautifully situated in the Ouse valley, this vineyard specialises in French-style wines rather than the more common German style.

Carr Taylor Vineyards, Yew Tree Farm, Westfield, Hastings TN35 4SG. Telephone: 01424 752501.
Open: January to Easter, Monday to Saturday; Easter to Christmas, daily.

Nearly 40 acres (16 hectares) of vineyard are available for visitors to follow a vineyard trail and visit the winery. The vineyards have been established since 1971 and the wines have won many prizes.

Chilsdown Vineyard, Old Station House, Singleton. Telephone: 01243 811398.

Based on the old Singleton railway station, this 13 acre (5.2 hectare) vineyard has eighteen thousand vines growing on the slopes of the Downs overlooking the village. There is a vineyard trail.

English Wine Centre, Drusillas Corner, Alfriston BN26 5QS. Telephone: 01323 870164.
Open: daily.

Situated in an old Sussex barn adjoining the vineyard and wine museum, this is the largest stockist of English wine in the country. There are guided tours for groups.

Hidden Spring Vineyard, Vines Cross Road, Horam TN21 0HF. Telephone: 01435 812640.
Open: daily.

There are 9 acres (3.6 hectares) of vines with a trail and guided tours are available by arrangement.

Leeford Vineyards, Whatlington, Battle TN33 0NQ. Telephone: 01424 773183.
Open: January to Easter, Monday to Friday; Easter to Christmas, daily.

Started in 1982, this is now one of the largest vineyards in the county with over 50 acres (20 hectares) under cultivation. Visitors can stroll through the vines and taste the wines in a converted oasthouse.

Lurgashall Winery, Windfallwood, Lurgashall GU28 9HA. Telephone: 01428 707292.
Open: daily.

The conversion of the old buildings housing the winery won a number of awards and they are of interest in their own right, quite apart from the wines. The winery specialises in country wines, meads and liqueurs and self-guided tours can be taken at weekends.

Merrydown Wine Company, Horam Manor, Horam. Telephone: 01435 812254.
Open: April to October, Tuesday to Friday.

One of the most famous English winemakers, Merrydown specialises in country wines and ciders. There is an audio-visual presentation, guided tours by appointment, and an opportunity to taste the products.

Nash Vineyards, Horsham Road, Steyning. Telephone: 01903 814054.
Open: June to October, daily.

There are 5 acres (2 hectares) of vines with a trail and tours by arrangement.

Nutbourne Vineyards, Gay Street, Nutbourne, Pulborough RH20 2HE. Telephone: 01798 815196.
Open: Easter to October, daily.

Over 18 acres (7.2 hectares) of vines are available for self-guided tours or guided tours by arrangement. The shop is housed in the old Nutbourne windmill.

Rock Lodge Vineyard, Scaynes Hill, near Haywards Heath. Telephone: 01444 831567.
Open: May to September, daily except Sundays.

There are 4 acres (1.6 hectares) of vines with a trail or guided tours by arrangement.

St George's Vineyard, Waldron, Heathfield TN21 0RA. Telephone: 01435 812156.
Open: March, weekends only; April to June and September to October, Tuesday to Sunday; July, August and December, daily.

At this very attractive vineyard visitors can stroll around the vines and visit the winery. There is even a chance to 'adopt a vine' and eventually receive a bottle of wine with your own label. There is a restaurant and a shop housed in a seventeenth-century barn.

Sedlescombe Vineyard, Cripp's Corner, near Battle TN32 5SA. Telephone: 01580 830715.
Open: Monday to Saturday.

This was the first organic vineyard in Britain and offers a vineyard trail and wine tasting.

11
Folklore, customs and events

Sussex is rich in legends and folklore; stories of ghosts, dragons, giants and the Devil and his works are numerous.

Many natural features are associated with the Devil and, in particular, his constant battle with local saints. **Devil's Dyke**, near Brighton, is said to be the unfinished attempt by the Devil to breach the Downs overnight and flood the Weald and all its churches. He was foiled in this enterprise by St Cuthman, who made the cocks crow early, and an old lady who held up a candle behind a sieve to simulate the rising sun! At **Mayfield**, Satan, disguised as a young woman, tried to tempt St Dunstan, a blacksmith, who pinched the Devil's nose with red-hot tongs. With a mighty leap to Tunbridge Wells, the Devil cooled his nose in a spring which has tasted sulphurous ever since.

Dragons are reputed to have lived in **St Leonard's Forest**, and here the saint fought an epic battle with a dragon and killed it. It is said that wherever the saint's blood fell lilies-of-the-valley grow today. Another type of dragon, called a knucker, lived in bottomless pools, or knucker holes. These pools were found in many places and the dragon's hot breath ensures that they never freeze in winter. A famous knucker hole can be seen at **Lyminster** near Arundel.

Several giants have lived in Sussex, including one at **Brede** who ate children. The Long Man of **Wilmington** is said by some to be the outline of a giant killed on this spot by a hammer thrown by another who lived at Firle, and the legendary Bevis of Hampton, the subject of a fourteenth-century poem, had connections with Sussex.

Ghosts are numerous. Many occur in relation to historical events such as King Harold at **Battle**. Others are more recent and were connected with the smuggling trade, for example the ghostly drummer at **Herstmonceux**

Castle. Smugglers had a vested interest in keeping inquisitive eyes from certain places and many of the 'ghosts' were never seen again when the revenue men cleared up the smugglers.

Many of the old customs of the county are associated with religious holidays, or the agricultural year. When holidays were few and hours long, any excuse for a celebration was taken to relieve the monotony of everyday life. Since the Second World War once widespread customs have disappeared, or occur only locally. A number have survived and continue to flourish and the revival of interest in past customs has resulted in some becoming re-established. Besides these traditional events, many more recently established ones have been added to the Sussex calendar.

Many villages and towns have fetes and fairs, morris dancers, and so on; the following calendar of events includes only those which have more than a purely local interest.

January
International Chess Tournament at Hastings.
Plough Sunday Service at Chichester Cathedral on the Sunday nearest to Twelfth Night.

February
Pancake Race at Bodiam on Shrove Tuesday.

Easter
British Individual Marbles Championship at Tinsley Green on Good Friday.

April
Heathfield Fair on 14th; called Cuckoo Day, as the old lady who keeps the cuckoos over winter releases the first one at the fair.

May
Battle Festival.

Blessing of the Sea Ceremony at Hastings
Fish Market on the Wednesday before
Ascension Day.
Festival of Arts at Brighton.
International Show Jumping at Hickstead.
Mayfield Festival (biennial).

June
Glyndebourne Festival Opera.
International Ladies' Tennis Championship
at Eastbourne.
International Show Jumping at Hickstead.
Horse-racing at Goodwood.
South of England Show at Ardingly.

July
Charleston Manor Music Festival.
Chichester Festivities: seventeen days of
artistic events based around the cathedral.
Ebernoe Horn Fair on St James's Day; a
cricket match on the village green and a
whole sheep roasted – the match winners
receive the horns as a trophy.
Glyndebourne Festival Opera.
Horse-racing at Goodwood and Brighton.
International Show Jumping at Hickstead.
Petworth Festival.

August
Arundel Festival: one of the main events is a
performance of a Shakespeare play in the
castle grounds.
Champion Town Crier of England contest at
Hastings.
Glyndebourne Festival Opera.
International Dressage Championship at
Goodwood.
Westergate Country Fair at Angmering.

September
International Dressage Championship at
Goodwood.
Rye Festival.
Sheep fair at Nepcote Green, Findon, on the
second Saturday of the month.
Wine Festival at the English Wine Centre,
Alfriston.

November
Bonfire Night celebrations at Lewes, Battle,
Rye and many villages.
Veteran Car Rally, London to Brighton, on
the first Sunday of the month.
Worthing Music Festival.

12
Tours for motorists

The following itineraries are based roughly on the ancient administrative divisions of Sussex,
the Rapes. They give a good impression of the variety of the scenery in the county and most of
the important places of interest will be visited.

Chichester, Fishbourne, Bosham, Uppark,
South Harting, Trotton, Fernhurst,
Blackdown, Lurgashall, Lodsworth,
Easebourne, Midhurst, Singleton, East Dean,
Goodwood, Boxgrove, Bognor Regis,
Pagham Harbour, Chichester.

Arundel, Littlehampton, Climping, Slindon,
Bignor, Fittleworth, Petworth, Wisborough
Green, Billingshurst, Pulborough, Amberley,
Arundel.

Bramber, Steyning, Shoreham-by-Sea, Worthing, Cissbury, Shipley, Horsham, Crawley,
Bramber.

Lewes, Rodmell, Piddinghoe, Newhaven,
Rottingdean, Brighton, Hove, Clayton,
Ditchling, Burgess Hill, Haywards Heath,
West Hoathly, East Grinstead, Sheffield
Park, Lewes.

Pevensey, Eastbourne, Beachy Head, Alfriston,
Seaford, Glynde, Ringmer, Uckfield,
Ashdown Forest, Crowborough, Mayfield,
Heathfield, Hailsham, Herstmonceux,
Pevensey.

Hastings, St Leonards, Bexhill, Battle,
Penhurst, Brightling, Burwash, Wadhurst,
Bewl Water, Ticehurst, Etchingham,
Robertsbridge, Northiam, Rye, Winchelsea,
Fairlight, Hastings.

13
Famous people

Many famous people have been connected with Sussex. A number of noble families have made their homes in the county, such as the Dukes of Norfolk at Arundel, the Dukes of Richmond at Goodwood, the Dukes of Devonshire at Eastbourne and the Nevilles, Sackvilles, Pelhams and Percys.

Soldiers, statesmen and politicians have lived in or been natives of Sussex, and the arts are well represented. Of authors, Edward Gibbon was a frequent visitor at Sheffield Park and is buried in Fletching church. William Cobbett travelled through and described much of the county in *Rural Rides*. John Evelyn, the diarist, went to school in Lewes and H. G. Wells attended the grammar school in Midhurst. Rye was the birthplace of the Elizabethan dramatist John Fletcher; Henry James lived there at Lamb House, which is now owned by the National Trust (page 86), and William Thackeray visited the town and set his unfinished novel *Denis Duval* there. The town was also the home of the American novelist Conrad Aitken and Malcolm Lowry, author of *Under the Volcano*, often stayed with him; Lowry is buried in Ripe churchyard.

Stephen Crane, author of *The Red Badge of Courage*, rented Brede Place; D. H. Lawrence rented a cottage at Greatham and wrote *The Rainbow* there; H. E. Bates was stationed at RAF Tangmere in 1942 (see page 104) and whilst there finished his novel *Fair Stood the Wind for France*.

The coastal resorts have attracted many writers and have been used as settings for numerous novels. Lewis Carroll spent his summer vacations in Eastbourne; Charles Dickens and Thackeray visited Brighton, as did Sir Arthur Conan Doyle, who later made his home in Crowborough. Shoreham-by-Sea is described, in his autobiography, by Evelyn Waugh, who was a pupil at nearby Lancing College. John Galsworthy spent his holidays at Littlehampton and lived at Bury; after his death in London his ashes were brought back to Sussex and scattered on the Downs above the village. Robert Tressell lived in Hastings and used the town as the setting for *The Ragged Trousered Philanthropists*.

Of others who made their homes in Sussex, Anthony Trollope lived at South Harting, Hilaire Belloc at Shipley, A. A. Milne at Hartfield; many of the Winnie-the-Pooh stories are set in Ashdown Forest (see page 58). Virginia Woolf lived at Monk's House, Rodmell (now owned by the National Trust; see page 87) until her tragic death in 1941 and Rudyard Kipling lived first at Rottingdean and later at Bateman's, also now owned by the National Trust (page 83). Sir Dirk Bogarde spent many holidays as a child at Littlington in the Cuckmere valley and started his acting career at Newick.

Of the naturalists, Gilbert White was a regular visitor to his aunt's house in Ringmer and wrote of her tortoise, Timothy, in his Selborne diaries; Timothy now has pride of place on the village sign at Ringmer. Richard Jefferies spent the last few years of his short life in Sussex and died at Goring-by-Sea; he is buried at Broadwater cemetery and nearby is his admirer W. H. Hudson, who wrote so lovingly of the Downs.

The poets are well represented: Shelley was born at Warnham, near Horsham; Charlotte Smith lived at Bignor Park; Walter de la Mare at Henfield; and Tennyson made his home on Blackdown (page 58). William Blake lived for a time at Felpham and it was here that he became involved in a dispute with some soldiers which resulted in his being tried, but acquitted, of sedition.

Painters have also found Sussex attractive: Thomas Blinks, the noted Victorian animal painter, lived at Ticehurst; Burne-Jones lived at Rottingdean and Rossetti was married at St Clement's church, Hastings. Turner was a frequent visitor to the county, particularly at Petworth and Brightling. Edward Stott lived at Amberley, Edward Burra at Playden, and Duncan Grant and Vanessa Bell lived at Charleston Farmhouse near Firle (see page 83). Rex Whistler stayed at the Old Ship in Bosham, then an exclusive club, and painted his last work on one of the walls two days before being killed on the beaches of Normandy in 1944.

Of composers, Frank Bridge was born at Brighton and died at Eastbourne; Sir Edward Elgar lived for some years near Fittleworth and wrote his Cello Concerto whilst there. Sir Arnold Bax made his home in Storrington and John Ireland, who entitled one of his compositions *Amberley Wild Brooks*, lived at Washington and is buried at Shipley a few miles away.

14
Tourist information centres

Arundel: 61 High Street, Arundel BN18 9AJ. Telephone: 01903 882268.

Battle: 88 High Street, Battle TN33 0AQ. Telephone: 01424 773721.

Bexhill-on-Sea: De La Warr Pavilion, Marina, Bexhill TN40 1DP. Telephone: 01424 212023.

Bognor Regis: Belmont Street, Bognor Regis PO21 1BJ. Telephone: 01243 823140.

Brighton: 10 Bartholomew Square, Brighton BN1 1JS. Telephone: 01273 323755.

Chichester: 29a South Street, Chichester PO19 1AH . Telephone: 01243 823140.

Eastbourne: 3 Cornfield Road, Eastbourne BN21 4QL. Telephone: 01323 411400.

Fontwell: Little Chef Complex, Junction A27/A29, Fontwell BN18 0SD. Telephone: 01243 543269.

Gatwick Airport: International Arrivals Concourse, South Terminal, Gatwick Airport RH6 0NP. Telephone: 01293 560108.

Hailsham: The Library, Western Road, Hailsham BN27 3DN. Telephone: 01323 844426.

Hastings: 4 Robertson Terrace, Hastings TN34 1EZ. Telephone: 01424 718888.

Hastings: *Fishmarket, The Stade, Hastings. Telephone: 01424 718888.

Horsham: 9 The Causeway, Horsham RH12 1HE. Telephone: 01403 211661.

Hove: Church Road, Hove BN3 3BQ. Telephone: 01273 778087.

Hove: King Alfred Leisure Centre, Kingsway, Hove BN3 2WW. Telephone: 01273 746100.

Lewes: 187 High Street, Lewes BN7 2DE. Telephone: 01273 483448.

Littlehampton: *Windmill Complex, Coastguard Road, Littlehampton BN17 5LH. Telephone: 01903 713480.

Lower Dicker: Boship Roundabout (A22), Lower Dicker, Hailsham BN27 4DP. Telephone: 01323 442667.

Peacehaven: Meridian Centre, Roderick Avenue, Peacehaven BN10 8BB. Telephone: 01273 582668.

Pevensey: Pevensey Castle, High Street, Pevensey BN24 5LE. Telephone: 01323 761444.

Rye: Heritage Centre, Strand Quay, Rye TN31 7AY. Telephone: 01797 226696.

Seaford: Station Approach, Seaford BN25 2AR. Telephone: 01323 897426.

Worthing: Chapel Road, Worthing BN11 1HL. Telephone: 01903 210022.

Worthing: *Marine Parade, Worthing BN11 3PX. Telephone: 01903 210022.

Asterisks* indicate centres that are not open throughout the year.

Index